THE MORTGAGE MANUAL

THE MORTGAGE MANUAL

Don DeBat and Thomas A. Kelly

CONTEMPORARY BOOKS
CHICAGO · NEW YORK

Library of Congress Cataloging-in-Publication Data

DeBat, Don.
 The mortgage manual.

 1. Mortgage loans—United States.   2. House buying—
United States.   I. Kelly, Thomas A. (Thomas Alfred)
II. Title.
HG2040.5.U5D423   1989   332.7'22   89-25199
ISBN 0-8092-4252-4

Copyright © 1989 by Don DeBat and Thomas A. Kelly
All rights reserved
Published by Contemporary Books, Inc.
180 North Michigan Avenue, Chicago, Illinois 60601
Manufactured in the United States of America
Library of Congress Catalog Card Number:
International Standard Book Number: 0-8092-4252-4

Published simultaneously in Canada by Beaverbooks, Ltd.
195 Allstate Parkway, Valleywood Business Park
Markham, Ontario L3R 4T8 Canada

CONTENTS

	INTRODUCTION...................................vii
CHAPTER 1	A SURVIVAL COURSE IN BIG-LOAN HUNTING..1
CHAPTER 2	SOURCES OF MORTGAGE MONEY..............7
CHAPTER 3	INTEREST RATES: WHY ARE THEY SO VOLATILE?..............15
CHAPTER 4	HOW MUCH HOUSE CAN YOU AFFORD?.....21
CHAPTER 5	ALL THE COSTS OF HOME OWNERSHIP....35
CHAPTER 6	HOW TO START SHOPPING FOR A MORTGAGE..45
CHAPTER 7	READING THE FINE PRINT....................57
CHAPTER 8	THE 30-YEAR, FIXED-RATE MORTGAGE.....67
CHAPTER 9	THE 15-YEAR LOAN: A SHORTCUT TO HOME OWNERSHIP........73
CHAPTER 10	THE BIWEEKLY MORTGAGE....................79
CHAPTER 11	FHA LOANS: HOW UNCLE SAM HELPS CASH-STRAPPED BORROWERS...............84
CHAPTER 12	HOW VETERANS CAN BUY WITH LITTLE OR NO MONEY DOWN.................91

CHAPTER 13	MORTGAGE BOND FINANCING: POPULAR AND ENDANGERED	*97*
CHAPTER 14	ADJUSTABLE-RATE MORTGAGES: A CHANGE IN THE RULES	*102*
CHAPTER 15	GRADUATED-PAYMENT LOANS AND OTHER INNOVATIVE MORTGAGES	*112*
CHAPTER 16	MORTGAGES FOR THE ELDERLY	*120*
CHAPTER 17	CREATIVE FINANCING	*130*
CHAPTER 18	PARENTS HELP OUT	*140*
CHAPTER 19	COMPUTERIZED MORTGAGE HUNTING: THE WAVE OF THE FUTURE	*149*
CHAPTER 20	TWENTY COMMON QUESTIONS AND ANSWERS ABOUT HOME LOANS	*152*
APPENDIX:	LOAN AMORTIZATION AND LOAN PROGRESS TABLES	*162*
	ABOUT THE AUTHORS	*169*
	INDEX	*171*

INTRODUCTION

Since the first edition of *The Mortgage Manual* was published in 1986, there have been a number of changes affecting mortgage markets and home buyers. To keep readers up to date, sections of the book have been rewritten, a chapter added, and tax information updated.

The first major change in the book involves income tax laws and rules. In 1986, the highest marginal tax rate was 50 percent, and there were nine other marginal tax rates for married couples filing joint returns, depending on their taxable income. The updates in Chapter 5 reflect the change to a maximum tax rate of 28 percent or 33 percent and only one other rate of 15 percent. In addition, the standard deduction for couples who itemize on their tax returns is $5,200 for 1989 and higher in the future. For singles, it's $3,100 in 1989.

The book also has been updated to reflect the higher loan limits allowed by most lenders who sell loans in the secondary mortgage market. In 1989, the maximum mortgage amount is $187,600, up substantially from the $133,250 of 1986. For most borrowers, the new maximum is plenty.

Another important change to the book is the addition of a chapter that explains how parents can help children buy a home. In the last few years, parental help has become crucial for many first-time buyers. Chapter 18 suggests a number of ways that parents can structure financial aid to help their offspring across the threshold of a home.

The book still contains information about the advantages and disadvantages of a number of mortgage types. It also suggests which mortgage might best suit a particular buyer.

In addition, Chapter 20 contains 20 frequently asked questions and their answers, which go a long way in helping readers understand the home-buying process.

THE MORTGAGE MANUAL

CHAPTER 1

A SURVIVAL COURSE IN BIG-LOAN HUNTING

Before venturing into the uncharted territory of today's mortgage market, home buyers need to pass a consumer survival course in big-loan hunting.

Whether you are shopping for your first home, moving up to a bigger house, or hunting for a retirement residence, cutting a path through the Mortgageland jungle can be financially perilous for the unwary.

Home-loan interest rates in the late 1980s became affordable again. However, rising housing prices have partially offset the rate decrease. Many young people still find it a challenge to save a large enough down payment and to qualify for a mortgage.

In 1949, the average homeowner spent 14 percent of his earnings on mortgage payments. Today, it takes at least 28 percent of the average homeowner's gross income just to meet the monthly mortgage payment and pay real estate taxes and insurance. Two of every three first-time buyers need two incomes to make the mortgage payments.

In 1982, when home loan rates averaged about 15 percent, buyers needed an annual income of $44,743 to qualify for a $72,000, fixed-rate, 30-year loan. The monthly payments for principal and interest would have been $911.

Mortgage Payments and Income Needed to Buy a $100,000 Home

Use this chart to estimate the minimum income you need to qualify for the monthly payments on a $100,000 home. A 10 percent down payment of $10,000 is assumed and monthly principal and interest (P&I) payments are based on a $90,000 mortgage for 30 years. Annual taxes and homeowners' insurance payments (T&I) are estimated at 2 percent of the purchase price, or $2,000. For simplicity, private mortgage insurance is ignored. The total monthly payment for principal, interest, taxes, and insurance (PITI) is exactly 28 percent of the minimum qualifying annual income.

Interest Rate	Monthly P&I	Monthly T&I	Total PITI	Annual Income to Qualify
8%	$661	$167	$828	$35,486
9	725	167	892	38,229
10	790	167	957	41,014
11	858	167	1,025	43,929
12	926	167	1,093	46,843
13	996	167	1,163	49,843
14	1,067	167	1,234	52,886
15	1,138	167	1,305	55,929

Rate decreases to a range of 9 percent to 11 percent in the late 1980s were offset somewhat by higher prices, but a window of opportunity still opened for some home buyers. A purchaser who bought a $120,000 house, placed 10 percent down, and grabbed a 10 percent mortgage for 30 years qualified for a $108,000 loan with income of $49,200 (assuming property taxes and homeowners' insurance amounted to 2 percent of the purchase price). Monthly principal and interest payments alone would be $948 a month. If interest rates were still at 15 percent, the monthly payment would be a hefty $1,366 on the $108,000 loan.

IS HOME OWNERSHIP WANING?

Rising home prices and the historically high interest rates of the early 1980s caused the rate of home ownership in the United States to level off—even drop—for the first time since the Great Depression.

After steadily increasing since the 1930s, home ownership peaked in the third quarter of 1980 when 65.8 percent of the nation's residents owned their own home, according to the U.S. Bureau of the Census. In 1988, only 64 percent of Americans—a decrease of more than a million households—owned their own home.

This trend has been most apparent among young households, especially those headed by persons under 30 years of age. In 1981, 41.3 percent of Americans in this age group owned their own home. In 1988, the figure was 35.9 percent, the census bureau reports.

But if you're among the one-third of Americans who don't own a home, don't despair. It still is possible to buy, now that rates are down on their continuing roller coaster ride.

THE HOME-OWNING MAJORITY

If you are old enough to remember World War II, radio thrillers, and the Brooklyn Dodgers, you've probably long forgotten the worry of saving for a down payment and applying for a mortgage on your first home.

Even if you bought your home in the era of 5 percent fixed-rate mortgages, lend an ear. The rules of the mortgage game have changed and continue to change. Someday soon you may want to swap that 1950s ranch in suburbia for a retirement condo in Florida, and then you'll understand why so many young buyers look so bewildered.

A few years ago, taking out a home loan was as easy as a Sunday stroll at the zoo. By merely visiting the local bank or savings and loan association, filling out an application, and passing a credit check, borrowers were well on their way to owning the American dream.

However, you can't use yesterday's assumptions in today's mortgage market. Today, all borrowers—young, old, and in between—must educate themselves so they can track down a mortgage that meets their needs. This book will introduce you to the most popular types of home loans now available and explain how they work.

While most buyers today are applying for old-fashioned fixed-rate mortgages—the plain vanilla variety of home loan—don't make up your mind until you have studied all the options.

OLD-FASHIONED MORTGAGES

Conventional fixed-rate mortgages feature an interest rate and monthly payment that do not change over the course of the loan, usually 15 or 30 years. A new twist offered by some lenders allows payments every other week, which means you can pay off the loan faster, saving thousands of dollars in interest. But the biweekly mortgage has been slow to catch on.

The typical fixed-rate mortgage is set up so that the interest portion of each monthly payment decreases over time, while the principal portion increases. The total payment each month stays the same.

Another fixed-rate loan possibility is the government-backed mortgage. Home loans backed by the Federal Housing Administration and Department of Veterans Affairs are much like conventional fixed-rate loans. FHA and VA loans, however, allow lower down payments and can be assumed by the next owner of the home.

NEW BREED OF HOME LOANS

Whether you are a first-time buyer or a seasoned homeowner looking for a retirement home, there are many new types of mortgages that you may want to study. Unfortunately, these loans often complicate the rules of the mortgage game.

For example, in the early 1980s, thousands of borrowers in the United States took adjustable-rate mortgages (ARMs), but experts say many of them don't understand how the payment or rate adjustments are made.

Basically, an ARM is a loan with an interest rate that can change as often as specified. Some may change every six months, some every year or every three or five years. Interest-rate adjustments are tied to some financial index—the rate on one-year U.S. Treasury bills, for instance. If the rates on T-bills go up, so does the rate on your mortgage. On some ARMs, this may affect your monthly payment. On others it may affect the length of the mortgage or your equity in the home.

For young buyers who have low current income but high earning potential, there are other innovative financing options. For example, payments on growing-equity mortgages (GEMs) and graduated-payment mortgages (GPMs) are designed to increase with the borrower's income.

Older homeowners can take out a mortgage without buying a home. That's because a reverse-equity mortgage converts the equity in their home into cash.

Balloon loans and buying on contract aren't popular when mortgage rates are affordable, but these loan options thrive when interest charges are high.

Clearly, all these options make the unsophisticated borrower easy prey for the creatures that prowl Mortgageland. The jungle path to home ownership is no Sunday stroll, but this book should help borrowers cut their way through the complicated choices, seesawing interest rates, special fees, and processing delays.

CHAPTER 2
SOURCES OF MORTGAGE MONEY

Until a few years ago, more than half the money for America's home loans came from savers' deposits in savings and loan associations (S&Ls), mutual savings banks, and other thrift institutions.

Today, however, savings institutions' mortgages often are sold to investors. And giant mortgage companies have staked claims to a substantial share of the market. This, too, has changed how home buyers go about getting a mortgage.

Through the mid- to late 1970s, S&Ls paid low interest rates on their large, insured savings deposits, and many states regulated the maximum interest rate that could be charged on a home loan. Maximum rates paid to savers also were regulated by states or the federal government, so thrift institutions had the cheapest money to lend and were the most active in financing private homes.

Federal tax regulations are structured to encourage thrifts to invest at least 80 percent of their assets in mortgages for residences.

However, in the early 1980s, the arrival of volatile interest rates and the deregulation of financial institutions turned the home-loan market upside down.

As regulations on savings and lending were phased out, depositors shopped around for the best return on their savings, often moving their money out of the thrift institutions. With less inexpensive money to lend, the lenders turned increasingly to capital markets for funds with which to make mortgages.

START AT AN S&L

Despite market changes and the woes of some savings and loan associations, your local S&Ls still are a good place to start your search for a home loan. These institutions still specialize in long-term mortgages within their service area.

Generally, S&Ls are more sensitive to borrowers' needs because they want to service the loans and maintain a good customer relationship. However, you may pay a slightly higher rate at an S&L, because few of them handle the volume of business that industry leaders and mortgage firms accommodate.

When the mortgage market is booming, a borrower who deals with an S&L may have his or her loan processed and approved faster than at a mortgage company. Often appraisers and credit and survey companies try to get a major S&L's work done as quickly as possible, because the thrift institution sends them so much business. Mortgage companies may handle more loans, but they often are spread throughout the country, not just in one city or county.

Most S&Ls will lend up to 95 percent of a home's appraised value, so qualified borrowers can get a mortgage with as little as 5 percent down. S&Ls often give preferential treatment to borrowers who have accounts with them already.

S&Ls offer a wide variety of financing plans, but to protect themselves against inflation, many institutions encourage home buyers to choose adjustable-rate mortgages. Because this type of loan allows lenders to raise rates when inflation increases, S&Ls usually offer ARMs at initial rates about 1.5 to 2 percentage points below a comparable fixed-rate loan.

If the thrift institution is federally chartered and regulated, it can offer all federally approved loan plans, including ARMs and graduated-payment mortgages.

Although thrift institutions hold billions of dollars of mortgages in their portfolios, they have increasingly sold loans into the secondary mortgage market.

By using secondary market organizations such as the Federal Home Loan Mortgage Corporation as a conduit, S&Ls sell fixed-rate loans to investors, thus reducing the potential for being stuck with old 8 percent loans, for example, when other lenders are charging 10 or 11 percent.

Though this practice may seem to have little impact on borrowers—who continue to send monthly payments to the lender—it does allow lenders to make more loans than otherwise possible. A more detailed discussion of the secondary market can be found later in this chapter.

In addition, a number of large S&Ls have set up mortgage subsidiaries to handle that part of their business. The only difference you may notice is the company's title.

COMMERCIAL BANKS

Another major source of mortgage money is commercial banks, which actually concentrate most of their efforts on serving business clients. Most of the funds in commercial banks come from short-term checking and savings accounts, and much of their mortgage activity involves loans for offices and business and construction loans.

But much as some appliance dealers specialize in microwaves, while others rely on washers and dryers, some banks take a more active role in residential mortgages. Banks generally are permitted to lend up to 75 percent of the value of the property. That means you'll need a 25 percent down payment to qualify. Don't expect to find great bargains at most commercial banks, because their mortgage rates usually are on par with or even slightly higher than those at S&Ls. But it never hurts to compare rates.

MORTGAGE BANKERS AND BROKERS

If you obtain a home loan from a mortgage banking company, the firm probably will sell your loan to an investor and use the proceeds to make new loans. But the company will continue to collect your monthly payments and service your loan. Unlike an S&L, however, the mortgage company probably is not based in your town or even in your state.

Mortgage banking companies make their money on loan origination fees and any profit they can make from selling the loans in the secondary market to institutional investors, such as life insurance companies or pension funds.

These aggressive loan brokers will make conventional residential mortgages, and some firms specialize in FHA and VA loans because these secure, government-backed mortgages are easy to sell to investors.

Often, mortgage companies offer the most competitive rates in town, because they deal almost directly with investors. But these lenders often charge higher points than S&Ls.

During the hot real estate market of the mid-1980s, mortgage bankers and brokers came under heavy criticism in some states because of processing delays, which caused interest-rate commitments to expire before loans were closed. Thousands of consumers paid hundreds of dollars each to "lock in" rates and then ended up paying higher rates and more points because interest charges had increased since they had applied. The protection of locked-in rates was a mirage once the rate commitment had expired.

Mortgage companies said single-digit interest rates created a stampede that buried appraisal, survey, and credit companies in an avalanche of work. There was nothing they could do, the firms said, although some offered to cancel loan applications, refund fees not yet spent, and turn over completed credit report, survey, and appraisal papers to the borrowers.

Although S&Ls also experienced delays, many institutions honored their expired commitments because they wanted to maintain good customer relationships. S&Ls had more flexibility than mortgage firms because at least some of their loans are made with savers' deposits.

Mortgage brokers and bankers were caught in a squeeze because their loans already were sold to investors. When rate commitments expired and interest rates moved higher, mortgage companies could pass the new market rate on to borrowers or take a loss on the loans.

CREDIT UNIONS AND PENSION FUNDS

Nearly two-thirds of the 58 million credit union members nationwide can get the money to purchase, refinance, or borrow against a home through their credit union. There are more than 16,000 federal- and state-regulated credit unions in the United States, and many of them have the financial capacity to make home loans.

Even credit unions with less than $2 million in assets may write residential mortgages without prior approval from the National Credit Union Administration. In the past, credit unions have specialized in short-term consumer loans.

Traditionally, credit unions offer better deals on consumer loans than banks and loan companies. Now, it also is possible to obtain an affordable mortgage through a credit union.

For example, Chicago-based United Air Lines Employees' Credit Union, the nation's second largest credit union with 83,000 members, will make home loans without charging discount points or an application fee. United will make 20-year adjustable mortgages at 1.25 percent over the prime lending rate.

Pension funds are loaded with cash that could be used for mortgages. For example, the AFL-CIO union pension fund holds $50 billion of the nation's $80 to $90 billion total assets in multi-employer pension plans.

Because pension funds seek a secure, fixed rate of return for their participants, mortgages may be an ideal investment for them. The U.S. Labor Department has given limited approval for pension plans to offer their participants residential mortgages at below prevailing rates. Because of regulation changes, pension funds soon could become like mortgage companies and fund home loans.

THE SECONDARY MARKET

The secondary market, which links lenders to capital markets, is the fastest growing segment of the home mortgage business.

Sources Of Mortgage Money

  This dramatic growth is not apparent to the average borrower, who may never realize his or her mortgage was sold by an S&L, bank, or mortgage company. The homeowner whose mortgage is sold through the secondary market continues to make monthly payments to the original lender, which services the loan for the investor.

In its early development, the secondary market helped financial institutions shift funds from regions of the country where there was extra mortgage money to areas where available cash couldn't meet demand.

As the secondary market developed over the past decade, it has become an important mechanism for increasing the flow of funds from Wall Street's bond markets to Main Street's mortgage needs. In doing so, it helped develop standardized mortgage instruments.

A number of players make up the secondary market. These include the Federal National Mortgage Association, the Government National Mortgage Association, and the Federal Home Loan Mortgage Corporation.

Established by Congress to buy FHA loans in 1938 when credit was scarce, FNMA (Fannie Mae) is the largest single investor in residential mortgages. It became a private, for-profit corporation in 1968 and began buying conventional loans in 1970. Acting like a giant savings and loan association, Fannie Mae buys mortgages from lenders and packages them into securities for investors.

The Government National Mortgage Association (GNMA, or Ginnie Mae) was established as an arm of the U.S. Department of Housing and Urban Development in 1968 to provide secondary-market support for the government's housing programs. It buys FHA and VA mortgages, pools them into securities, and then sells them to investors.

The Federal Home Loan Mortgage Corporation

(FHLMC, nicknamed Freddie Mac) was established in 1970 to provide a secondary market for conventional loans. Much of its business is with savings and loan associations. Freddie Mac packages its loans in pools and sells participation certificates to investors.

In addition to these major secondary market corporations and associations, home loans also are sold by mortgage brokers to S&Ls, insurance companies, pension funds, and other investors.

So, through S&Ls, banks, mortgage companies, credit unions, and pension funds, today's home buyer has a potpourri of mortgage sources from which to choose. With the help of more standardized mortgage instruments and the tremendous liquidity created by the secondary mortgage market, even novice home-loan hunters should be able to find the funding they need.

CHAPTER 3

INTEREST RATES: WHY ARE THEY SO VOLATILE?

Everything has a price, and a mortgage is no exception. The interest rate—or price—of a home loan is determined in the marketplace, where money is borrowed and lent.

In the mid-1980s, fixed rates on long-term mortgages dropped below 10 percent for the first time in the decade, creating a boom of home sales and a stampede of refinancing activity. Although rates climbed back to the 10 percent to 11 percent range at the end of the decade, many experts expect them to decline again in the 1990s.

To understand the roller coaster nature of home-loan rates, you have to look back over five or six decades. Mortgage rates have come a long way since the 1920s, when home buyers were required to make 50 percent down payments and finance the balance with a balloon loan that was due in full—or could be refinanced—after five years.

When many of the balloon loans came due during the Great Depression of the 1930s, millions of borrowers couldn't afford to pay them off. They lost their homes.

In 1934, Congress created the Federal Housing Administration to encourage home ownership in the United States. The FHA created the first government-backed long-term home loans that could be paid off in affordable monthly installments.

In those days, lenders charged 3 percent to 4 percent annual interest on home loans. It wasn't until inflation started to heat up in the 1950s that all interest rates, including those on mortgages, began their gradual climb. By the early 1960s, lenders were charging 6 percent on 30-year, fixed-rate mortgages.

THE TIGHT-MONEY ERA

Mortgage rates began to increase faster in the early 1970s. At the beginning of the decade, mortgage rates were in the range of 7 percent to 8 percent. A recession, the oil crisis, and the tight-money period of 1973-74 sent rates up to 9 percent. During the housing boom years of 1975-78, rates again stabilized at a new plateau in the 8 percent to 9 percent range.

At the beginning of the 1980s, deregulation of the banking industry prompted many substantial changes. Limits were lifted on interest rates that lenders could offer to depositors. State laws that limited the rates lenders could charge for loans were wiped off the books. As mentioned earlier, mortgage lenders now could compete for funds with commercial banks, businesses, and the federal government.

Unfortunately, deregulation, soaring inflation, and the recession of 1980 coincided to send an interest-rate tremor stronger than the eruption of Mount St. Helens through the home finance market.

Record high interest rates of nearly 20 percent resulted from inflationary pressures generated in the

American economy through "two decades of reckless spending by Congress and the attempt of our government to try to penalize the industrious and reward the indolent," said Merrill Butler, 1980 president of the National Association of Home Builders.

When inflation was running at 9 percent and 10 percent, Butler said, "It doesn't make any difference whether mortgage rates are 15 percent or 18 percent—you can only kill a man once. And we were killed off when rates started going above 13 percent."

In Illinois, one of the states hit hardest by the housing recession, mortgage rates hit a record 17.5 percent in spring of 1980. In New York and California, home loan rates peaked in the 17 percent to 18 percent range.

By summer 1980, the crunch eased and mortgages were available at about 11.5 percent to 12 percent in most sections of the nation. But by year's end, rates bounced back to the 14 percent to 16 percent range.

At 16 percent interest—the prevailing rate nationwide at the end of 1980—only 4 out of every 100 families in America could afford to carry a $60,000 mortgage for 30 years.

Mortgage lending was down to a trickle. Several of Chicago's top savings and loan associations reported hefty losses in 1980, and a third of the home builders in the area left the business.

The skyrocketing rates and deregulation also spurred use of the adjustable-rate mortgage. ARMs allow lenders to increase or decrease the interest rate—and usually a borrower's monthly payment—based on the movement of previously agreed-upon indexes.

After deregulation, lenders declared that the fixed-rate, long-term mortgage was dead. They said the volatile marketplace made it impossible for them to lock in rates for 20 or 30 years. Instead, they said, mortgage rates would have to vary with economic conditions. They warned that S&Ls couldn't stay in business long with their money lent out on 8 percent mortgages for 20 more years and current savers being paid 12 percent on certificates of deposit.

Forecasters said mortgage rates of 9 percent would never be seen again in our lifetime. Their crystal balls must have been clouded by their own short-sightedness.

REBIRTH OF FIXED-RATE LOANS

In the recovery years of 1983 and 1984, charges on fixed-rate mortgages gradually declined to 12 to 14 percent. (See the chart on page 17.) By 1985, fixed-rate mortgages were available at 11 percent. A wide variety of ARM loans at *initial* discounted rates of 8 to 10 percent also were available.

Deeply discounted single-digit ARMs enjoyed a brief popularity in 1983-85. At one point, lenders boasted that ARMs accounted for half their new loan business. Consumers didn't fare too badly either. With an initial rate of 10 percent, for example, a borrower was paying perhaps 3 percentage points less than a fixed-rate loan would require. The only risk was that rates might increase.

But by the mid-1980s, borrowers were dancing on their loan-repayment books. For the first time in more than seven years, long-term, fixed-rate home loans again were available in the 9 percent to 10 percent range. Some 70 percent of the home loans originated in 1986 carried fixed rates as home sales soared and refinancing began to gather steam.

What caused interest rates to tumble?

Most economists agree that Reaganomics' curbing of inflation brought down all interest rates. After several years of inflation at far less than 5 percent a year, even the most cynical observers began to believe that double-digit price increases wouldn't return quickly.

History of Fixed-Rate Mortgage Interest

Here is a list of long-term effective interest rates charged by savings institutions over the years for conventional loans on new homes. This chart was compiled by the U.S. League of Savings Institutions from figures gathered by the Federal Home Loan Bank Board.

Year	Rate
1965	5.81%
1970	8.45
1971	7.74
1972	7.60
1973	7.96
1974	8.92
1975	9.00
1976	9.00
1977	9.02
1978	9.56
1979	10.78
1980	12.66
1981	14.70
1982	15.14
1983	12.66
1984	12.37
1985	11.58
1986	10.75
1987	10.51
1988	10.70
1989	11.05*

*(Six-month average)

In 1988, with the election of President George Bush, inflation and interest rates began to rise. Near the end of the decade, borrowers again were paying 11 percent on a 30-year fixed mortgage, and ARMs were starting out at more than 9 percent.

RATES AND OIL PRICES

The decline in oil prices also played a major role. In the 1970s, soaring oil prices were blamed for the surge in interest rates. Experts say the decline in oil prices reinforced the notion of economic stability. Passage by Congress of the Gramm-Rudman Act, which aims to curb deficit spending, also gave a psychological lift to those who doubted that balancing the budget was really a goal of the Reagan administration.

Also, the Federal Reserve Board helped bring interest rates down with a monetary policy that allowed enough money to flow into the system to keep the economy moving but—the Fed hoped—not enough to create an inflationary condition in which too many dollars chase too few goods.

So, investors and bank depositors are accepting sharply lower interest rates for their money. As a result, lenders can afford to reduce their rates on new mortgages. They still can maintain a profit margin between the interest they pay out and what they charge.

Lenders also have been freed of some of the risk in making long-term, fixed-rate home loans because a strong secondary mortgage market has been created.

Another phenomenon helping lenders is the growing popularity of 15-year, fixed-rate loans. Because the loans are for shorter terms than 30-year loans, the lender has more of its money back sooner. This reduces the impact inflation will have on the loans.

CHAPTER 4

HOW MUCH HOUSE CAN YOU AFFORD?

Home buying, especially in a boom market, can be feverish and frightening. First-timers and experienced buyers alike start out with sweaty palms.

With For Sale signs and furnished models swirling in their heads, house hunters wonder what the best buys are: A vintage condo or a two-flat close to transportation in the city? A new single-family home or a town house in a fast-growing suburb?

Before you dive headfirst into the house hunt, you should know how much home you can afford. Buying a home usually involves coming up with a substantial cash down payment and qualifying for a mortgage to cover the balance of the purchase.

You should know the amount of down payment you'll need, and where you'll get it. You'll need to know how big a mortgage you can obtain and have some idea about the other costs of home ownership. You must have these facts and figures to be able to compute how much house you can afford.

The down payment will vary depending on the way the transaction is structured and the type of financing you obtain. Conservative lenders require 20 percent of the purchase price as a down payment on a conventional loan. On a $100,000 house, you would have to have $20,000 in cash. However, if you have good credit and enough income, and if the house is worth the price, most lenders will take a 10 percent down payment, or $10,000 on that $100,000 house.

If you qualify for an FHA loan, the minimum down payment is only 3 percent to 5 percent. However, you also will have to pay a government mortgage insurance premium. Check the FHA loan maximum in your area. In big cities such as New York or San Francisco, it's $101,250, but it is substantially less in smaller towns. If you are a veteran of the U.S. armed services, it is possible to obtain a Veterans Administration–guaranteed loan with no money down.

CASH FOR CLOSING
Sources for Down Payment Cash

Take a minute here to calculate how much money you have available for closing costs and a down payment. Your down payment has a direct relationship to the price of home you can afford and the type of financing you should seek.

The following worksheet will help you outline the available assets and funds you have to tap for your down payment:

Savings $_____

Equity in present home (minus selling costs) _____

Equity in other property _____

How Much House Can You Afford?

Investments (current value) _____
Life insurance (cash value) _____
Cash from relatives _____

Total available funds $_____

From this total amount, you will have to pay closing costs. Also, it's wise to set aside money for moving expenses, new furniture, and repairs or rehab costs that often arise during the first year in a new home. You also may want to keep some cash in case of emergencies.

It is an excellent idea for a home buyer to hire an independent engineer or home inspector to check the property for termites and potential structural and mechanical defects. This usually costs $250. Attach a rider assuring the inspector's approval to the sales contract on the house. The rider is a stipulation that the offer is based on the home passing inspection.

Private Mortgage Insurance

If your down payment is less than 20 percent, the lender will require you to pay a premium for private mortgage insurance (PMI).

By paying PMI, the borrower is protecting the *lender* for the difference between the down payment and 20 percent of the home's price, in case of default. Don't confuse PMI with life insurance; PMI merely protects the lender.

With a 10 percent down payment, you would have to pay 0.4 percent of the mortgage amount at closing to cover the first year's premium. On the $90,000 mortgage, that's $360.

The second year's PMI with a 10 percent down payment will be 0.34 percent of the loan balance, but you will pay it during the first year because the premium is due at the beginning of the second year. On the $90,000 loan, it would be about $300—paid in 12 monthly installments of about $25, said Curt Culver, senior vice president of marketing for Mortgage Guaranty Insurance Corp., Milwaukee, Wisconsin.

If you place a 5 percent down payment, the initial insurance premium is 1 percent of the loan amount, or $950 at closing on the $90,000 mortgage. The second year's PMI would be 0.49 of the loan balance, payable in 12 monthly installments. That's about $39 a month.

On a 15 percent down payment, the initial insurance premium is 0.30 percent of the loan amount, or $245 at closing. In the second year, PMI would be based on 0.29 percent of the loan balance, or about $25 a month.

In addition, PMI can be paid in a lump sum at closing on loans with 10 or 15 percent down. The premium is 2.95 percent of the mortgage amount on a 10 percent down payment and 2.30 percent on a 15 percent down payment.

The PMI premium is held in escrow by the lender and paid to the mortgage insurance company at the beginning of each year.

Traditionally, PMI payments continue until you have paid off enough of the mortgage to reach 20 percent equity of the purchase price. In 1989, however, the Federal Home Loan Mortgage Corporation, which packages mortgages for the secondary market, began allowing lenders to consider a home's appreciation after only two years.

Not considering appreciation, however, it would take about nine years to reach 20 percent equity after making a 15 percent down payment on a $100,000 home with a 30-year fixed-rate mortgage. With 10 percent down, it would take 12 or 13 years. With a 5 percent down payment, it would take 15 years—half the mortgage's length. That's because the lion's share of early-year mortgage payments goes to interest, not principal.

Don't Overlook Closing Costs

Many first-time buyers—and those homeowners who bought homes before points became so prevalent—tend to overlook closing costs. But they are a major expense and can drastically cut into your down payment nest egg.

The largest closing cost usually is points, or special loan fees lenders charge to increase their profits. One point equals 1 percent of the mortgage amount. So, if a lender charges three points on a $90,000 mortgage, you will have to pay $2,700 at closing.

Some lenders will lower the interest rate on a loan if you will pay more points at closing. It is unusual today to find a lender willing to charge no points without raising the annual rate. Also, if you want to lock in the interest rate being offered at the time you apply, you usually will have to pay 0.5 to 1 point.

Points will make the annual percentage rate (APR) of your loan appear higher than originally quoted on the loan documents. You'll learn more about APR in Chapter 7.

In addition to the down payment and points, you may have to pay other major closing costs on a conventional loan. However, some of the charges listed may not apply to your transaction:

Loan Application Fee. Typically $250 to $300, the loan application fee usually covers the cost of the appraisal and credit report.

Loan Origination Fee. Expect to pay 1 percent of the loan amount, or $900 on a $90,000 loan, for a loan origination fee if you want to lock in the interest rate on your mortgage. If you float the rate and take the market level at closing, you won't pay this fee. The fee is like a point in every way but one: It's not tax-deductible.

Private Mortgage Insurance. If you put less than 20 percent down, you will have to prepay the first private mortgage insurance premium at closing. If you place 5 percent down, the first year's fee would be 1 percent of the loan amount. With 10 percent down, the fee would be 0.4 percent of the mortgage amount. If you put down 15 percent, the fee would be 0.30 percent.

Initial Mortgage Payment. The lender will require a buyer to pay the first month's mortgage payment at closing. On a $90,000 loan for 30 years at 10 percent, that would be $790.

Title Search and Insurance. The cost for a title search and insurance typically runs about $400, although part of the cost is tied to the home's price. The title policy, usually issued by a title insurance company, assures payment to any claimant in case of discrepancies in the title to the property. If you are buying a home, the fee usually is paid by the seller or split between buyer and seller.

Property Survey. A current survey, which costs $75 to $150, checks property lines to make sure that there are no encroachments on your land that might hamper a future sale. Usually it is paid for by the seller.

How Much House Can You Afford?   27

Deed Recording. This fee of $25 to $35 covers legally recording a deed with the proper governmental authorities.

Recording Taxes. Some local governments charge a stamp tax based on the amount of the sales transaction. A typical amount is $250.

Document Preparation. All that paper shuffling, including notary services, costs money. Figure about $50.

Prepaid Homeowner's Insurance. Generally, the lender requires the buyer to pay the first year's homeowners' insurance premium at or before closing. The cost is $250 to $400.

Prorated Property Taxes. If you buy a house and close on June 30, for example, you will be responsible for half of the year's taxes and insurance. If the seller already paid these costs for the whole year, he or she will get a rebate from you at closing. If this year's property taxes are payable next year, you will receive a prorated credit from the seller at closing.

Lawyer Fees. The attorney's fees will be about $250 to $500. Expect to pay higher legal fees on a condominium closing because of the added paperwork.

Closing Cost Summary

Once you have a home picked out, use this handy checklist to tally up actual closing costs.

Loan application fee	$_____
Loan origination fee	_____
Private mortgage insurance	_____

Initial mortgage payment   _____
Title search and insurance   _____
Property survey   _____
Deed recording   _____
Recording Taxes   _____
Document Preparation   _____
Prepaid homeowners' insurance _____
Prorated property taxes   _____
Lawyer fees   _____
  Total $_____

If you pay normal points and closing costs and don't lock in your mortgage rate, total closing costs on a $90,000 loan could easily be more than $4,000. When you add that to the $10,000 down payment, that's an out-of-pocket expense of $14,000 to step across the threshold of a $100,000 home.

Of course, substantial tax benefits are associated with home ownership. Details of the savings will be discussed in the next chapter.

FINANCING

Qualifying for a Mortgage

When figuring how much housing debt you can comfortably carry, the lender depends largely on two factors: the interest rate on the loan and your income.

The mortgage amount, term, and interest rate determine your monthly loan payment. The higher the interest rate, the higher the monthly payment. Your gross monthly income, less any substantial debts such as a car payment, determines how much you can spend for a mortgage.

Lenders have general rules of thumb. They say your mortgage principal and interest payments should not exceed 25 percent of your gross monthly income. When real estate taxes and homeowners' insurance are added, your monthly payments for principal, interest, taxes, and insurance (PITI) should not exceed 28 percent of your gross income. Total housing costs plus other long-term debts, such as car payments, student loans, and credit-card obligations, should not exceed 33 percent of the buyers' total gross monthly income.

If you can qualify within these guidelines, you should be able to afford a home. However, some families prefer to take on payments well below the maximum allowed.

These qualification standards usually serve both the borrower and the lender, helping both avoid a situation that could lead to a default.

What Can You Afford?

Before you buy a house and take on the burden of home-loan payments, you should calculate the maximum monthly mortgage payment you can afford and the total amount of down payment you have, less closing costs. These figures will help you figure the size of your mortgage and how much house you can afford.

Use the following mortgage worksheet to calculate how much house you can afford. The bottom line, maximum purchase price, will tell you how expensive a house you can qualify for.

When computing your gross monthly income, don't forget other sources of cash. Do you earn cash from a steady part-time job? Do you earn interest and dividends on investments, or make money on rent or leases?

Figure the mortgage payment you can afford:

If you know your family's gross monthly pay, write it on Line (1). If you don't know it, multiply gross weekly pay (before deductions) by 4.33. The result is gross monthly income.
Gross monthly income = weekly pay
_____ × 4.33 = $_____ (1)

Lenders say your monthly mortgage payment for principal and interest cannot be more than 25 percent of your gross monthly income. Multiply the amount on Line (1) by 0.25. The result is the payment you can afford.
Gross monthly payment you can afford =
Line (1) _____ × 0.25 = $_____ (2)

For simplicity, we are assuming that your monthly payment for taxes, homeowners' insurance, and PMI will be about 3 percent of your gross monthly income.

Net monthly payment you can afford:

Now that you know how much you can afford to pay, take a look at the payment tables on pages 33 and 34 to see how large a 15-year or 30-year fixed-rate mortgage you can handle. To use the tables, you need to know the current range of interest rates (look in your local newspaper or call a lender or two).

Choose the table for a 30-year loan (page 34) or a 15-year loan (page 33). Look across the line with the prevailing interest rate until you find a monthly payment near what you can pay. If the table does not go high enough for your income, a more complete table can be found in the Appen-

How Much House Can You Afford? 31

dix. Then, look up to the top of the chart to find the mortgage amount.

Enter this amount—the maximum
   mortgage amount—on Line (3). $_____ (3)

Gross cash available:

  Now that you know the mortgage amount you can afford, figure out how much you will have to pay in closing costs. That will let you know how much is left for a down payment.

On Line (4), enter the total amount of
   cash you have set aside for the down
   payment, inspection fee, moving
   expenses, repairs, emergencies, and
   closing costs: $_____ (4)

Subtract $250 for the home inspection fee.
   Enter the answer on Line 5:
Line (4) _____ − $250 = $_____ (5)

Subtract from Line (5) the money you
   will keep for moving expenses, initial
   home repairs, and emergencies. Enter
   the answer on Line (6):
Available funds = Line (5) _____ −
_____ = $_____ (6)

Multiply the mortgage amount from Line
   (3) by 0.045, the average total closing
   costs. Enter your estimated total closing
   costs on Line (7):
Closing costs = Line (3) _____ ×
0.045 = $_____ (7)

Net cash available for down payment:

To find net cash available for down payment, subtract closing costs on Line (7) from the available funds on Line (6). Enter amount available for down payment on Line (8):

Amount available for down payment =
Line (6) _____ – Line (7)
_____ = $_____ (8)

Maximum home cost—the bottom line

To figure the maximum purchase price of a home you can afford, add the maximum mortgage amount from Line (3) and the maximum down payment from Line (8). Enter the answer—the maximum purchase price—on Line (9):

Maximum purchase price = Line (3)
_____ + Line (8) _____ = $_____ (9)

Payments for Principal and Interest on a 15-Year Mortgage

Principal Amount

Interest Rate	$50,000	$60,000	$70,000	$80,000	$90,000	$100,000	$120,000	$150,000
8.5%	$492	$592	$689	$787	$886	$984	$1,171	$1,476
9.0	507	609	710	811	913	1,014	1,217	1,521
9.5	522	627	731	835	940	1,044	1,253	1,566
10.0	537	645	752	860	967	1,075	1,290	1,612
10.5	553	663	774	884	995	1,105	1,326	1,658
11.0	568	682	796	909	1,023	1,137	1,364	1,705
11.5	584	701	818	935	1,051	1,168	1,402	1,752
12.0	600	720	840	960	1,080	1,200	1,440	1,800
12.5	616	740	863	986	1,109	1,233	1,479	1,849

Payments for Principal and Interest on a 30-Year Mortgage

Principal Amount

Interest Rate	$50,000	$60,000	$70,000	$80,000	$90,000	$100,000	$120,000	$150,000
8.5%	$384	$461	$538	$615	$693	$ 771	$ 923	$1,153
9.0	402	483	563	644	724	805	966	1,207
9.5	420	505	589	673	757	841	1,009	1,261
10.0	439	527	614	702	790	878	1,053	1,316
10.5	457	549	640	732	823	915	1,098	1,372
11.0	476	571	667	762	857	952	1,143	1,428
11.5	495	594	693	792	891	990	1,188	1,485
12.0	514	617	720	823	926	1,029	1,234	1,543
12.5	534	640	747	854	961	1,067	1,281	1,601

CHAPTER 5

ALL THE COSTS OF HOME OWNERSHIP

A mortgage payment is only part of the cost of home ownership. So far you've figured out roughly how much you can afford to pay for a house.

Once you find a specific home you are interested in, the worksheets in this chapter will help you estimate all housing costs, including utilities and maintenance. Perhaps you should skim this chapter now and return to it once you have a specific house in mind.

If you have a budget like this one ready, you'll be fairly well-prepared for a qualifying interview at the bank, savings and loan association, or mortgage broker.

MONTHLY HOUSING COSTS

Use the following six-step guide included in this chapter and the handy loan amortization tables in the Appendix to estimate total monthly housing payments, including principal and interest payments, real estate taxes, homeowners' insurance, monthly utility bills, and maintenance costs.

Monthly Mortgage Cost Per Thousand Dollars

This table shows the monthly cost of borrowing per $1,000 at various interest rates.

Interest Rate	15-Year Loan	30-Year Loan
8.0%	$ 9.56	$ 7.34
8.5	9.85	7.69
9.0	10.15	8.05
9.5	10.45	8.41
10.0	10.75	8.78
10.5	11.06	9.15
11.0	11.37	9.53
11.5	11.69	9.91
12.0	12.01	10.29
12.5	12.33	10.68
13.0	12.66	11.07
13.5	12.99	11.46
14.0	13.32	11.85
14.5	13.66	12.25
15.0	14.00	12.65

First fill in this basic information:

Home purchase price $_____
Mortgage amount (principal minus down $_____
   payment)
Mortgage interest rate   _____%
Term of loan   _____yrs.

All The Costs Of Home Ownership

STEP 1

To determine loan amount in thousands, divide the mortgage amount by 1,000 and enter the result on Line (1).

Loan amount _____ ÷ 1,000 = _____ (1)

In the table on page 36, find the cost per $1,000 for your mortgage's interest rate and term. (For example, if the rate is 10 percent and the term is 30 years, the cost per $1,000 is $8.78.)

Enter the cost per $1,000 on Line (2): _____ (2)

To find the monthly principal and interest payment, multiply mortgage amount (in thousands) from Line (1) by the cost per $1,000 from Line (2). Enter the answer on Line (3):

Monthly payment = Line (1) _____
×
Line (2) _____ = _____ (3)

STEP 2

To figure monthly cost for the property tax, enter annual property taxes and divide by 12. Enter your answer on Line (4):

Annual taxes _____ ÷ 12 = _____ (4)

STEP 3

To figure monthly homeowners' insurance costs, enter the yearly cost of homeowners' insurance and divide by 12. Enter your answer on Line (5):

Annual insurance _____ ÷ 12 = _____ (5)

STEP 4

Estimates for the home's monthly heating, electricity, water, and garbage pickup bills should be available from the seller. Telephone costs should be based on your current expenses. Enter this information on the following lines:

Natural gas or oil	_____ (6)
Electricity	_____ (7)
Water	_____ (8)
Telephone	_____ (9)
Garbage collection	_____ (10)
Total utilities = total of lines (6), (7), (8), (9), (10) =	_____ (11)

STEP 5

A rule of thumb is that annual maintenance costs equal about 1 percent of the home's price. To estimate yearly maintenance and repairs, multiply the home's sale price by .01. The monthly expense is that amount divided by 12. Enter the monthly amount on Line (12).

Price _____ × .01 ÷ 12 =   _____ (12)

STEP 6

Now let's put those monthly housing costs together. Add the following figures:

Mortgage payment from Line (3)	_____
Property taxes from Line (4)	_____
Insurance costs from Line (5)	_____
Utility costs from Line (11)	_____
Maintenance costs from Line (12)	_____
Add these amounts to get the bottom line, total monthly home ownership costs:	$_____ (13)

HOME BUDGET WORKSHEET

Now that you know what it will cost to put a roof over your head, it's time to look at some of your family's other spending habits and preferences. This will give you a bottom-line assessment of whether you'll be eating franks and beans every night for the privilege of owning a home.

Average monthly nonhousing expenses
Food _____
Clothing _____
Transportation, including car costs _____
Life insurance _____
Health insurance _____
Medical and dental care _____
Education _____
Installment payments _____
Savings, emergency funds _____
Entertainment and recreation _____
Vacations _____
Charity _____
Pocket money _____
Other: _____

Total nonhousing expenses $_____ (14)

Now add your total monthly nonhousing expenses to your total monthly housing expenses from Line (13).
Line (13) _____ + Line (14)
_____ = $_____ (15)

Compare the total on Line (15) to your total monthly take-home pay. If you are signing up to shell out more than you bring in, relax for a minute. The U.S. Congress knows it's expensive to be a homeowner. So realizing that homeowners also are voters, the good people in Washington, D.C., created income tax deductions that make this whole situation a lot easier to take.

COMPUTING INCOME TAX SAVINGS

The true out-of-pocket cost of owning a home can't really be computed until you deduct income tax savings from your monthly payment. After all the tax changes passed by Congress in 1986, home buyers and owners still enjoy three substantial deductions.

First, points paid separately at closing are deductible from federally taxable income in the year paid. This is a one-time fee and a one-time deduction. The other two major tax advantages of home ownership—the deductibility of mortgage interest and property taxes—provide annual assistance.

The amount of tax savings created by the deductions is based on the individual homeowner's tax bracket. Of course, your actual monthly payments do not change. The savings come once a year at income tax time from the deductions you claim.

For example, let's suppose a married couple in the 28 percent tax bracket took out a $90,000 mortgage. (Based on 1989 tax rates, they would have a joint taxable annual income of $30,950 to $74,849.)

The couple paid $2,700 in points to close their $90,000 mortgage. Assuming they file a joint tax return, they could deduct the full $2,700 from their 1989 income, providing a tax savings of $756. Similarly, they could deduct 28 percent of their mortgage interest payments and property taxes, so their annual tax savings would be substantial.

All The Costs Of Home Ownership 41

Use the following guide to estimate what the *real* monthly cost will be for your home after allowable tax deductions:

STEP 1: Figuring your monthly tax deduction

To estimate monthly tax deductions on mortgage interest, multiply the monthly principal and interest payment from Line (3) by .97. (That's because at least 97 percent of your first-year payments is tax-deductible.) Enter answer on Line (16):

Line (3) _____ × .97 = _____ (16)

Enter your monthly property tax payment on Line (17): _____ (17)

To figure total monthly deductions, add Lines (16) and (17). Enter your answer on Line 18:

Line (16) _____ + Line (17)
_____ = _____ (18)

STEP 2: Figuring your tax savings

To figure your monthly tax savings, multiply your monthly tax deductions from Line (18) by your marginal tax rate. To find your tax rate, look under the appropriate filing status in the tax table on page 43. For example, a couple filing jointly with annual income of $55,000 has a tax rate of 0.28. Enter your answer on Line (19):

Monthly tax savings = Line (18)
_____ × tax rate _____ = _____ (19)

STEP 3: After-tax housing cost

To figure your after-tax monthly housing cost, subtract your tax savings on Line (19) from your total monthly home ownership costs on Line (13). Enter the answer on Line (20):

Line (13) _____ − Line (19)

_____ = _____ (20)

STEP 4: Total after-tax monthly cash outlay

To figure your after-tax monthly cash outlay, add your after-tax monthly housing costs on Line (20) to your total nonhousing expenses on Line (14). Enter your answer on Line (21):

After-tax monthly outlay = Line (20)

_____ + Line (14) _____ = _____ (21)

This table shows marginal tax rates for various amounts of taxable income. Numbers are provided for married couples filing joint returns and for single persons.

Note that the tax rates and brackets are for 1989. Check with the Internal Revenue Service for numbers applicable to future years.

As mentioned before, the deductions are taken only once a year at tax time. (The illustration here uses monthly tax saving to make the impact easier to see.) You have to pay out the amount on Line (13) each month. You probably would be wise to reduce the amount withheld from your paycheck for federal income tax so you can meet your bills.

Despite keeping tax advantages for homeowners, the 1986 tax changes have made it more difficult to benefit

Marginal Tax Rates

Married Couples Filing Joint Returns		Single Persons	
Taxable Income	Tax Rate	Taxable Income	Tax Rate
$0–$30,949	15%	$0–$18,549	15%
$30,950–74,849	28%	$18,550–$44,899	28%
$74,850–$155,319	33%	$44,900–$93,129	33%
$155,320+	28%	$93,130+	28%

from the deductions. So, the preceding worksheet may be an oversimplification—and perhaps an overstatement—of the benefits.

Here's how it works. First, fewer items are deductible on Schedule A of your 1040 form. Second, the threshold at which the deductions help you is much higher. Until the last couple of years, you could deduct state sales tax and 100 percent of all consumer interest. By 1991, you will be able to deduct no state sales tax and no interest paid on anything except loans secured by your home. Also, the thresholds you must reach with items such as medical bills and union dues have been raised, eliminating these deductions for most people.

As a result, the total itemized deductions for families are hundreds or thousands of dollars less than several years ago, even if a family's situation is exactly the same. That means you may end up using mortgage and property tax deductions just to reach the threshold at which they'll do some good.

Also, that threshold—the standard deduction—for couples filing jointly is up to $5,200 in 1989. In other words, the first $5,200 in deductions—which are now harder to get—does a family absolutely no good. For singles, the standard deduction is $3,100.

With state income taxes, property taxes, mortgage interest, and charitable deductions as the major deductions for most families, many homeowners—especially middle-income families—are finding that the deductions aren't as large as they expected.

Still, itemizing makes sense, but it is less productive than in past years. To determine what this would mean for you, work through a Schedule A. Forms are available from the IRS by calling 1-800-424-3676.

CHAPTER 6

HOW TO START SHOPPING FOR A MORTGAGE

The early 1990s look like a good time to buy a home. Although home prices are increasing, interest rates are relatively stable in most cities around the country.

There's no telling if or when long-term fixed rates will dip below 9 percent again, but if you've been watching the housing market during the past few years, you know that today's rates are far better than what was available early in the 1980s.

If you completed the worksheet in Chapter 4, you know how much house you can afford. Once you decide to buy a home, selecting the right type of mortgage for your pocketbook and qualifying for it constitute the next step.

"In the good old days, the head of the neighborhood savings and loan would look you over with a squint. If you looked like an all-right guy, he'd make the loan," said Chicago real estate lawyer Marshall J. Moltz. "Today, the borrower is a voice on a telephone, and there are many more financial requirements and approval documents. Everything is fed into a computer, and applying for a mortgage is much more impersonal."

As Moltz points out, seeking a loan has changed dramatically. In fact, shopping for a home loan today is like scanning the menu at a fancy French restaurant. Lenders not only have a wide assortment of products to peddle, but some of their offerings may seem foreign to you. So it pays to know your way around the mortgage marketplace before you start.

SHOP AROUND

The amount you pay each month for your home mortgage depends, in part, on the type of mortgage you select and the prevailing interest rate. But it also can be affected by the lending institution you choose.

One lender may charge a slightly lower rate than another for an identical mortgage. Another might charge a slightly higher rate, but fewer points. Application fees and other closing costs for similar loans also can vary from lender to lender.

So, if you are short on cash for a down payment, choose the lender who charges a slightly higher rate, but fewer points. Because you are spending such a large amount of money, it is essential that you shop around—comparing rates, terms, and closing costs—before choosing a mortgage and a lender.

Lenders are eager to make mortgages, because loans generate new fee and servicing income. And, lenders say, borrowers who finance homes at today's lower rates usually are better credit risks and less likely to default than those facing the 15 percent rates of the early 1980s.

THE LOAN RUSH

When loan rates are low—especially after extended periods of substantially higher rates—mortgage makers tend to be very busy. In early 1986, when mortgage rates tumbled to nearly 9 percent from more than 12 percent a year earlier, millions of Americans rushed to buy houses or refinance high-interest home loans.

But the magic of single-digit interest rates created a stampede that buried appraisal, survey, and credit companies in an avalanche of work. Three months after applying for a loan, some borrowers still hadn't been able to close their deals.

If loan applications are pouring in, you might be put on a waiting list just for an appointment. Getting an appraisal of the home—necessary for the lender—can take five to ten weeks, instead of the two weeks usual in a normal housing market.

A credit report, usually issued in days, can take five weeks during a mortgage boom, and a property survey that usually takes one week can take six times as long. Heavy application volume in the mid-1980s caused some lenders to extend interest-rate commitments to 75 days on a conventional loan and 90 days on government-insured mortgages. In a normal year, the total process can be completed in 30 to 45 days.

In the mid-1980s, borrowers complained that some mortgage brokers let rate commitments expire, then increased rates to reflect recently increased interest charges. But mortgage bankers and brokers said they had no choice. Investors wanted the highest yields possible and refused to honor expired commitments for single-digit mortgages when higher rates were available.

Since then, however, the demand for loans has receded, and stories of long delays have become less common. Conscious of the image problems created, a number of lenders have introduced plans that feature loan approval within a week or two.

In addition, some lenders are touting low-documentation mortgages. These "low-doc" loans usually require down payments of at least 30 percent, but some of the paperwork—including employment verifications—is skipped, speeding the process along.

WHERE TO START THE HOME-LOAN HUNT

Mortgage experts give the following home-loan shopping list for families starting the mortgage hunt:

Look in your own backyard. Based on the mortgage brokers' track record in 1986, some analysts recommend paying a slightly higher rate and going to a bank or S&L, which likely will be more customer oriented.

Begin at your neighborhood S&L or bank. It could prove to be the best place to get a loan, especially if you are an established customer. If you are not a customer, become one. Most lenders want to keep their loyal customers.

However, don't assume your lender has the best deals. Check around. Some lenders charge higher rates because they aren't all that interested in home mortgages.

Don't be overanxious. Don't get locked into accepting the first loan you're offered without making certain it's the best available at the time. With the frequent fluctuation of rates these days, no lender has the best deal even half the time.

Shop around. Although it may be fun to shop for bargain prices on consumer products, it can be even more rewarding if you take the time to find a mortgage deal. Get quotations from at least three lending institutions, and preferably many more. A few extra phone calls could save you hundreds of dollars.

For example, if you inquire at a bank or S&L around April 15—right after the federal income tax deadline—you might find the institution loaded with cash from Individual Retirement Account deposits. In farm communities, a lender may be flush soon after harvest.

If you find an eager lender, you may be able to negotiate a lower mortgage rate, and there also may be lower point charges. Even a reduction of 0.25 percentage points in the interest rate can represent a savings of thousands of dollars over the life of a fixed-rate loan.

Compare more than just interest rates. Ask what other charges you will have to pay. These could include points, loan origination fee, application fee, appraisal fee, and many more charges. And don't forget to ask friends and business associates about the lender's reputation. In 1986, some lenders earned dubious achievement awards for bumbling mortgage processing and allowing delays that cost borrowers thousands of dollars in fees and higher monthly payments.

Consider shorter mortgages. Don't be afraid of shorter-term loans. When fixed rates are low, thousands of borrowers take on shorter-term loans.

Picking a 15-year loan over a 30-year loan will mean higher monthly payments, but the savings on interest could amount to tens of thousands of dollars, and the gain in equity will be substantial. On a $50,000 loan at 10 percent for 15 years, you would owe $40,650 after 5 years. Had you chosen a 30-year loan at 10 percent, you would owe $48,300 after 5 years.

The difference is even more dramatic after 15 years. You would be holding a mortgage-burning party for that 15-year loan, but you'd still owe $40,850 on the 30-year mortgage. (To find out the equity buildup with each loan, see the mortgage progress table in the Appendix.)

Beware of rate fluctuations. It is important to ask exactly when the rate you are applying for will be established. With rates fluctuating daily, a homeowner should determine whether the contract rate will be the one available on the day of the application or the one available on the day of the actual closing.

Some lenders may charge up to a full point extra if a homeowner wants to lock in a rate. When rates are stable or moving lower, it is a good idea to apply for a loan and let the rate float until closing. There's no sense in paying to lock in a rate when interest charges may go lower.

Ask questions. It pays to inquire about different loan programs because lenders now are offering so many new types of mortgage instruments. The programs vary from one institution to another. But don't accept a loan you don't want. If a bank or S&L says it will give you only an adjustable-rate mortgage, and you don't want that, go elsewhere.

Don't forget to ask about government-backed loan programs. Ask your realty agent if the house you plan to buy is eligible for an FHA-insured loan. Eligibility depends on a maximum price level by geographic region. For example, the maximum in New York and Chicago is $101,250, but it's only $95,000 in some Chicago suburbs. If you or your spouse served in the military, you may be eligible for a no-money-down Veterans Administration–guaranteed loan.

Mortgage lenders have more types of loans to offer than ever before, but many of them may not be for you. Pros and cons of some of the most popular home financing options available at S&Ls, banks, and mortgage companies will be discussed starting in Chapter 8.

Don't wait forever. In every interest-rate cycle, some borrowers want to wait until rates hit bottom. Don't worry about getting the absolutely lowest rate. Experts say borrowers should cut their financing deal when rates are in the trough of the cycle—not when they start to head up.

When even Wall Street's wizards can't figure how low—or high—rates will go, the best advice is to take a deal that makes financial sense. Your rate may not be absolutely the lowest, but you will have a home you can afford. And the price tomorrow is likely to be higher.

MORTGAGE QUIZ REQUIRES HOMEWORK

The lender you select will have two basic questions: First, can you come up with the down payment for the mortgage? Second, can you afford the monthly payment, including principal, interest, taxes, and homeowners' insurance?

The boom housing market and refinancing craze buried lenders under a mountain of mortgage applications in 1986. When rates are affordable, borrowers must work harder to help lenders get their loan approved.

Of course, lenders will ask how much money you need to borrow and for how long. But there also will be questions about your monthly income, bank balance and debts, age, marital status, and number of dependents.

Getting Personal

Questions involving economics sometimes may seem personal to a sensitive applicant. For example, the home-loan application required by the Federal Home Loan Mortgage Corporation (Freddie Mac) and the Federal National Mortgage Association (Fannie Mae) ask the following penetrating questions:

1. Have you been declared bankrupt in the last seven years?
2. Are there any outstanding judgments against you?
3. Was your property foreclosed upon, or did you give title or deed in lieu of foreclosure?
4. Are you a co-maker or endorser on a note?
5. Are you obligated to pay alimony, child support, or separate maintenance?
6. Is any part of the down payment borrowed?

Another sensitive area is marital status. Lenders say that the traditional family unit—working husband, homemaker wife, and one or more children—is no longer traditional. In fact, this structure now comprises the minority of home buyers.

Loan underwriters and realty agents see all types of shared-housing situations and make no distinction among them. At times, people may become uncomfortable about disclosing their relationship with a co-buyer.

Again, this is an economic issue. If you are a co-buyer in a nontraditional relationship, it might be wise to consult with an attorney to determine the legal ramifications of the partnership and how title of the property should be held.

Under the law, certain personal questions are forbidden, including whether the applicant is a U.S. citizen, has a police record, or belongs to any clubs, social organizations, or trade or service organizations.

Questions the Borrower Should Ask

Don't let the lender ask all the questions. The dollars you owe can change for each mortgage option a lender offers. Of course, you should ask basic questions about application and loan origination fees, interest rate, loan term, points, down payment, mortgage amount, and private mortgage insurance.

But there are other questions you should ask. Make copies of the following list of questions, and use it as a guide when comparing various mortgages and lenders:

1. Will I be required to pay into a special escrow account each month to cover property taxes and homeowners' insurance? Will the account pay interest?
2. Can the original term of the loan be extended?
3. Is there a grace period beyond a payment's due date, and is there a late payment charge on monthly payments?
4. If I prepay principal, how do I know how much of each future payment is principal and how much is interest? Do I receive an annual accounting of principal owed?
5. Can the loan be assumed by another qualified borrower? Does the lender have the right, upon assumption, to raise the rate of interest or charge an assumption fee?
6. Do the terms of the loan permit me to borrow additional money on the mortgage after I have paid off part of the original loan?
7. If I must pay private mortgage insurance, when can I stop paying it? Will the lender alert me, or do I have to watch for it myself?
8. Will the loan be sold to someone else? If so, to whom will I send payments?

SPEEDING YOUR MORTGAGE APPROVAL

Experts say the best way to survive the tedium of mortgage qualification is to be prepared for everything when you visit the lender.

"Homeowners can help speed loan approval by carefully collecting the pertinent financial data and making sure the loan officer gets it quickly," said mortgage analyst Gary S. Meyers, president of Chicago-based Gary S. Meyers & Associates.

What to Bring

Here are some tips and a list of documents and financial information you'll need when you apply for a mortgage.

Your Checkbook. When you first apply, most institutions will charge $250 to $300 to process a loan application. The money goes for a credit report and appraisal. They often won't start the wheels moving until it's paid.

Credit Report. Before you apply for a loan, it's well worth the fee—usually $15 to $20—to hire a reputable credit reporting agency to conduct your credit check. This will alert you to any surprises or mistakes listed in your credit background.

And, while you are hunting for a lender, the credit work will be under way. When you apply for the loan, you can notify the lender that the report is completed. If you don't know of such an agency in your area, ask potential lenders which agency they use. Then contact the agency directly.

How To Start Shopping For A Mortgage

Employment Verification. You will be asked to sign a verification form that will be sent to your employer. The form verifies that you are employed in good standing. Know the name of a person at your company who verifies employment and alert him or her that an inquiry is coming. If you've been with your current company for less than two years, you should have the same information and personnel contact with your former employer.

Proof of Income. You will need your federal income tax returns for the past two years, especially if you are self-employed. When quoting current or expected income, be sure to include any commissions, bonuses, or regular overtime pay. Child support and alimony also should be shown, whether you give it or get it.

Bank Accounts. Ask your savings institution for a statement showing that you have enough cash for the down payment and closing costs in your account. You also will have to provide account or certificate numbers for your checking and savings accounts, as well as the addresses of the financial institutions.

It's also a good idea to list any stock or bond holdings, because they would increase your financial standing in the lender's eyes. Find out where the institutions give out credit information. It may be the main office, not at the branch office you usually deal with.

Credit Cards. Give account numbers of all your major cards. Make sure all accounts are current, and clean up any delinquencies before you apply for the loan.

Outstanding Loans. You must provide the account number and addresses of all lenders. This includes real estate and personal loans.

Previous Loans. If you've paid off other loans, including student loans, list them and the lender. Credit companies often lack the information and don't report loans that are paid off. Make sure you get credit for having paid off loans.

Copies of All Documents. When supplying a lender with information, do not send original documents; copies are acceptable. To avoid delays, any papers mailed should be sent with a return-receipt request and be addressed to a specific person at the lending institution.

Questionable Debts. If you have any questionable debts, or there are any special circumstances regarding your credit background, tell the loan officer. Anything out of the ordinary that shows up on your credit report must be explained. Make it as easy as possible for a busy loan officer to approve your mortgage.

Know the Limits

To help protect themselves—and the borrower—financial institutions across the nation have tightened their credit requirements and limited the total debt borrowers are allowed to carry and still receive loan approval.

The limits are now 28 percent of *gross* income for mortgage payments, including principal, interest, taxes, and homeowners' insurance, and 33 percent of total debt, including credit cards and auto loans. This means that if your gross income is $2,000 per month, the highest monthly mortgage payment you may qualify for is $560 per month. Your total monthly debt payment may not exceed $660 per month.

CHAPTER 7
READING THE FINE PRINT

Before you put your signature on the dotted line of a sales contract for a home and all those legal documents needed to take out a mortgage, ask a real estate lawyer or other expert to help you interpret the fine print.

Like most legally binding documents, sales contracts and mortgage papers contain complex terms that a bricklayer, junior executive, or astronaut might not understand.

SALES CONTRACT CLAUSES

The standard real estate contract used in most parts of the nation contains more clauses than most buyers and sellers realize. Most of the provisions are negotiable—from the selling price to who pays for the termite inspection.

Hassles abound in real estate transactions, because many buyers and sellers don't read the contract's fine print. For example, a young couple signed a contract to purchase a vintage home in an area that had been reassessed and hit with a hefty real estate tax increase. However, when the buyers read the sales contract, it called for the seller to prorate the taxes based on 110 percent of the last bill, and place that amount in an escrow account.

If it were not for a sharp-eyed real estate lawyer, the first-home buyers would have been stuck with paying the part of the seller's taxes that probably will exceed 110 percent of the last tax bill. The attorney probably saved the young home buyers several hundred dollars—more than what most lawyers would charge.

"The tax proration clause in the broker's standard sales contract wasn't helpful," said Chicago real estate lawyer Marshall J. Moltz. "What if the taxes go up 50 percent? It could have cost the unsuspecting buyers hundreds of dollars."

To protect inexperienced clients, Moltz said lawyers should include a tax reproration clause in the sales contract. Then, the seller's share of the taxes can be reprorated when the bill arrives. If there isn't enough money in the escrow account, the seller would be required to pay the difference.

Subject to Attorney Approval

All too few home buyers bother to hire a real estate lawyer before they sign a contract to purchase a house. Unfortunately, most real estate sales contracts are signed, sealed, and delivered before a lawyer sees them. But it doesn't have to be that way.

Ideally, a savvy buyer would have a lawyer draft a purchase contract before papers are signed. However, if the buyer writes "subject to attorney approval" on the contract when he or she signs it, the protection will be there.

Within three to five days, the buyer's lawyer can

refine the sales contract and add provisions that he or she would have included if given the chance to draft it originally.

After all, most of the fine print in a typical real estate sales contract is designed to protect the seller, not the buyer. Consequently you need a lawyer to study all that fine print and to add a few provisions that are on your side.

Experts say a buyer needs a lawyer before the closing, too. "What happens if the roof leaks or serious structural problems develop in the house? It's a real estate lawyer's job to put warranties in the contract so there is a legal basis for voiding the deal if defects occur after closing," said Moltz.

What to Cover

Your attorney should review, approve, and add necessary addenda to the contract to cover the following key points:

Tax Prorations. To compute accurate tax prorations, the buyer and seller must use the most recent tax assessment rate plus 10 percent. However, when the final installment of the tax bill is issued, the buyer and seller will reprorate the taxes and make any necessary cash adjustment.

Mortgage Contingency Provisions. If a buyer is unable to obtain a commitment for a mortgage, he or she is required to notify the seller in writing as soon as possible.

But if the buyer fails to notify the seller in writing within a certain time period, the seller should not infer that the buyer has a mortgage or has agreed to purchase the property without financing. This clause protects a buyer from losing his or her earnest money.

Plat of Survey. A survey is like an X-ray. The seller is responsible for furnishing a survey no more than six months old, showing that there are no undisclosed encroachments or easements involving the adjoining property.

The standard title insurance policy does not protect against encroachments, boundary line disputes, or anything else that could be disclosed by a survey and a property inspection.

Restrictions of Record. The buyer purchases the property only subject to restrictions of record. Although deed restrictions, such as zoning, covenants, easements, or special assessments are highly technical, buyers should be aware of them and review them in the contract.

Right to Inspect. After the contract and addendum from an attorney are signed, the purchaser has the right to inspect the property and all improvements on it. The seller may not refuse the buyer access to the property.

Evidence of Good Title. The seller must produce evidence of good title in the form of a title commitment policy. Lenders require a title commitment policy.

Building Maintenance. The seller must agree to keep the property, including the building and all other improvements, in good repair between the date of the contract and closing.

Warranty Against Defects. When a home is purchased, there is an implied warranty of habitability. On the date of closing, the seller must warrant that all mechanical systems (such as water, sewer, plumbing, heating, and electrical), as well as appliances included in the sale, are in working order. The premises also must be free of structural defects and termites or other insect infestation.

"When it comes to plumbing, I advise my clients to flush before they buy," said Moltz, who once represented a purchaser who bought a house with plumbing fixtures that were installed but not connected to the sewer system. "It's a good idea to hire a professional engineer or home inspector to check the house before you buy."

MORTGAGE FINE PRINT

Not all the fine print is in the sales contract. There are plenty of pitfalls in mortgage documents, too. For example, here is a sample *acceleration clause* taken from a mortgage contract:

> In the event any installment of this note is not paid when due, time being of the essence, and such installment remains unpaid for thirty (30) days, the Holder of this Note may, at its option, without notice or demand, declare the entire principal sum then unpaid, together with accrued interest and late charge thereon, immediately due and payable. The lender may without further notice or demand invoke the power of sale and any other remedies permitted by applicable law.

This legal jargon means if you are more than 30 days late with your mortgage payment, the lender can require you to pay immediately the entire unpaid balance of the loan. If you don't have the money, the lender could start foreclosure proceedings that eventually could lead to a sheriff's sale of your home.

Note the use of the words *without notice*. If this contract provision is legal in your state, this means you have waived your right to notice of a missed mortgage payment or delinquency or default.

So, if you go on vacation to the Bahamas and forget to mail your mortgage payment—or your check is lost in the mail—the lender can initiate action against you before you are told. The lender may even start to foreclose.

Legal Tip: Know whether your mortgage contract waives your right to notice. If it does, obtain a clear understanding in advance of what you're giving up. And consider having your attorney check state law to determine whether the waiver is legal. Also, have the attorney talk to the lender about eliminating such language.

Beware of Due-on-Sale Clauses

For years, due-on-sale clauses have been included in many mortgage contracts. They are increasingly being enforced by lenders when buyers try to assume a seller's existing low-rate mortgage.

If your mortgage document includes a *due-on-sale clause,* the lender has the right to require immediate repayment of the unpaid balance if the property changes hands. Here is an example of a typical due-on-sale clause:

> If all or any part of the Property or an interest therein is sold or transferred by the Borrower without the Lender's prior written consent . . . the Lender may, at the Lender's

option, declare all the sums secured by this Mortgage to be immediately due and payable.

In due-on-sale cases, the courts frequently have upheld the lender's right to increase the interest rate to the prevailing market level.

Legal Tip: Be especially wary when a home seller offers to let you take over an "assumable mortgage." If the mortgage has a due-on-sale provision, the assumption may not be legal. If the deal goes through, the lender could raise the rate to the current market level, and you could be liable for a monthly mortgage payment hundreds of dollars higher than you planned. You may be getting a loan that's more expensive than you can afford.

Annual Percentage Rate

Closing documents also can contain confusing information on interest rates.

When a home buyer applies for a mortgage and obtains a loan commitment, the federal Truth-in-Lending Act requires lenders to disclose the *annual percentage rate* (APR), or the total charge for credit stated as a percentage, calculated on an annual basis.

APR allows different types of mortgages to be compared equally and fairly. On an adjustable-rate mortgage, APR equalizes such variables as rate adjustments, buydowns, first-year discounts, and other factors that affect the cost of an ARM.

Let's suppose you buy a $100,000 home, put $10,000 down, and take out a $90,000 mortgage for 30 years at a fixed interest rate of 10 percent. Your monthly principal and interest payment would be about $790.

However, in addition to this payment, the lender charges you three points—or $2,700—in closing costs.

When these points are amortized over the life of the mortgage, your annual percentage rate on the loan actually is 10.37 percent, not 10 percent.

And, because your down payment is less than 20 percent, you are required to pay a private mortgage insurance premium of $360 the first year and a decreasing amount each year, beginning at about $300 until your equity in the house equals 20 percent.

PMI is considered part of APR. So, when those insurance premiums are added in, the interest rate on the loan jumps from 10.37 percent to 10.72. In other words, a 10 percent nominal mortgage rate actually could be closer to 11 percent when points and PMI are used to compute APR.

Disclosure Rules

The Truth-in-Lending Act and its implementing Regulation Z provide rules for consumer credit disclosures. Credit terms, including APR, must be printed "clearly and conspicuously" on the loan documents and in any advertisements.

Therefore, APR should be perfectly clear both to lenders and to borrowers. But it isn't. Depending on which savings and loan association, bank, or mortgage broker you talk to, some are eager to quote APR, and others aren't. Often, you will be quoted the annual interest and points separately.

"There isn't a conspiracy to withhold APR information from borrowers, but some loan officers do not compute it until the mortgage closes," said Chicago mortgage analyst Gary S. Meyers. "This is not a deceptive practice that the Federal Trade Commission should investigate. There is no plot to hide APR, and the Truth-in-Lending Act isn't being violated.

"The truth is some of today's home-loan programs

are so complicated that many lenders simply do not know how to accurately calculate APR," Meyers added. "How do you compute the APR on an adjustable-rate mortgage when the interest rate is discounted in the first year?"

For example, one Chicago S&L offered a 7.75 percent first-year rate on an ARM. Because the loan has an annual cap, or limit, of 2 percentage points per year on rate adjustments, the lender projected the second-year rate at a maximum of 9.75 percent.

According to the mortgage document, the rate can go no higher than 13.5 percent during the 30-year term of the loan. Rate adjustments will be based on the movement of a cost-of-funds index for federally chartered S&Ls. So what's the APR? According to the computer, it is 10.216 percent.

Chances are your lender isn't sure what causes that rate to be the APR. And that means you probably won't be.

"Don't ask me how to compute APR—there are 100 variables to consider," said Michael L. Allen, president of Crown Mortgage Company in Oak Lawn, Illinois. The firm has a computer hookup to the data bank of Mortgage Guaranty Insurance Corporation (MGIC), a private mortgage insurance company based in Milwaukee, Wisconsin.

"We tap into MGIC's computer via telephone. We feed mortgage data—the loan type, the interest charge, and other fees involved in computing APR—to MGIC through our terminal, and they give us the annual percentage rate in a printout. We pay a fee of $3 or $4 for each APR they compute."

Legal Tip: All lenders must use the same method of computing APR as defined by the Truth-in-Lending Act. So if the APR on your loan seems too high, ask the lender to recompute it.

As you can see, there can be many potential problems hidden in the fine print of mortgage documents. To blindly sign on the dotted line is the biggest mistake a novice borrower can make.

Even if you are a veteran of several real estate closings, experts recommend that you hire legal counsel to sort out confusing and unintelligible clauses found in most mortgage documents.

CHAPTER 8

THE 30-YEAR, FIXED-RATE MORTGAGE

30-Year Fixed at a Glance

Interest rate: May be initially higher than other types of financing, but is fixed for the life of the loan.
Rate adjustments: None.
Payment changes: None.
Term of loan: 30 years.
Maximum loan amount: $187,600, but lenders will make larger loans with slightly different terms.
Assumable: No.
Ideal for: First-time buyers.

If you are a home buyer shopping for a mortgage with stable monthly payments and long-term tax advantages, the 30-year, fixed-rate loan may be ideal for your pocketbook.

ADVANTAGES

The 30-year, fixed-rate mortgage has three notable advantages:

1. The biggest advantage is payment predictability.
2. There can be some hefty income tax write-offs in the early years of the loan, because the majority of early payments goes to interest charges.
3. Most lenders permit you to prepay the principal, allowing you in effect to shorten the term of the loan. But such prepayments are entirely up to you, because you are under no obligation to pay more than the monthly payments.

DISADVANTAGES

There are some disadvantages to consider as well:

1. Principal is paid down at a very slow rate, following the 30-year amortization schedule.
2. If you take out a loan at a high rate and interest rates fall, you will have the expense of refinancing if you want to take advantage of the lower rate.
3. If you sell your home, the buyer usually cannot assume the loan.

STABLE MONTHLY PAYMENTS

The so-called, old-fashioned, 30-year, fixed-rate loan originally was developed in the 1930s when long-term mortgages came into vogue.

The 30-Year, Fixed-Rate Mortgage

The beauty of the 30-year, fixed-rate loan is its stable monthly principal and interest payments. A home buyer who took out a $40,000, fixed-rate loan at 8 percent interest in the mid-1970s paid about $293 a month for principal and interest. Because of higher real estate taxes and insurance premiums, the monthly payment probably has increased, but the payment for principal and interest still is the same.

A few years ago, mortgage experts considered this type of loan a vanishing species because lenders had been burned by skyrocketing interest rates while they were holding older low-rate loans.

With long-term rates hovering near 16 percent, few borrowers could afford the payments required by a fixed-rate loan. Instead, they took adjustable-rate loans with low initial rates. As rates dropped in the mid-1980s, however, more borrowers qualified for 30-year, fixed-rate loans and snapped them up.

The loan is popular because it eliminates the problem of "payment shock"—the unpleasant surprise to a family's budget caused by rate and payment increases—that can occur with adjustable-rate mortgages.

A 30-year, fixed-rate mortgage is set up so that the interest portion of each monthly payment decreases over time, while the principal portion increases. So, in the early years of the mortgage, the vast majority of your monthly payment goes for interest. All this interest is deductible from income in figuring your federal income tax. In the last few years of the loan, most of your payment is for principal, which is not deductible. The total payment, of course, remains the same.

When interest rates reach 11 or 12 percent, the 30-year, fixed-rate loan tends to be more popular than its cousin, the 15-year fixed, because monthly payments are lower and more borrowers can qualify.

For example, the monthly principal and interest

payment on a $90,000 mortgage at 11 percent for 30 years is $858. If you took out the same loan for 15 years, the payment would rise to $1,023—a difference of $165 a month, or enough to meet your car payment.

IDEAL FOR MIDDLE-INCOME FAMILIES

Because the monthly payments are stable, 30-year, fixed-rate loans are most popular with young, middle-income families who have the necessary down payment, but are trying to keep home expenses to a minimum and don't want surprises.

You'll pay more interest on a 30-year loan than on the 15-year, but this is offset somewhat by the advantage of bigger tax deductions for mortgage interest. Also, equity buildup is slow with this type of loan.

For example, after five years of a 30-year loan at 10 percent interest, $966 of every $1,000 borrowed would still be owed. On a $90,000 loan, that means you still would owe $88,920. After 10 years, $909 of every $1,000 borrowed would still be owed—or $81,810 of that $90,000 loan. And, after 15 years, you'd still owe $817 of every $1,000 borrowed, or $73,530 of the $90,000 loan.

On a 15-year loan at 10 percent, after 5 years you'd owe $813 for every $1,000 borrowed, or $73,170 of the $90,000 loan. However, after 10 years, you would owe only $506 of each $1,000 borrowed, or $45,540, and after 15 years you'd own the home outright.

Although the fixed-rate loan has higher initial interest charges than the initial rate on many adjustable mortgages, it lets the borrower know exactly how much home-loan payments will be for the next 180 or 360 months.

Payments on adjustable-rate loans, or ARMs, can rise and fall with market conditions, leaving a homeowner guessing and worrying what his or her monthly housing expense will be. ARMs are discussed in detail in Chapter 14.

While the general characteristics of 30-year, fixed-rate mortgages are the same, slightly different variations are offered by S&Ls, banks, and mortgage companies.

In choosing among the various offerings, the borrowers should first consider their down payment. The conventional fixed-rate mortgage generally requires a down payment of at least 5 percent, though some lenders increasingly are asking 10 percent down, and 20 percent is preferred. If the down payment is less than 20 percent, private mortgage insurance is required.

The Federal Housing Administration-insured fixed-rate mortgages allow a down payment of as little as 3 percent to 5 percent. Eligible veterans can obtain a Veterans Administration-guaranteed loan with no money down. FHA and VA loans will be covered in detail in Chapters 11 and 12.

LOAN MAXIMUMS VARY

If you take out a 30-year fixed at an S&L, bank, or mortgage company, your conventional fixed-rate loan probably will have a maximum amount of $187,600. That maximum is set by securities dealers who pool the loans into mortgage-backed securities, which are sold in the secondary mortgage market.

If you're moving to a dream home and hunting for a loan larger than $187,600, most S&Ls, banks, and mortgage companies offer a jumbo conventional loan. Amounts of $250,000 to $350,000 for 30 years at prevailing interest rates are fairly common. On occasion, even $1 million mortgages can be taken out. Unfortunately, most of us don't have to worry about such loans. Minimum down payments usually are 10 percent to 20 percent of the price.

CHAPTER 9

THE 15-YEAR LOAN: A SHORTCUT TO HOME OWNERSHIP

15-Year Fixed at a Glance

Interest rate: Fixed for the life of the loan and lower than on a 30-year, fixed-rate mortgage.
Rate adjustments: None.
Payment changes: None.
Term of loan: 15 years.
Maximum loan amount: $187,600, but lenders will make larger loans with slightly different terms.
Assumable: No.
Ideal for: Financially established second- and third-home buyers who expect to stay in their house at least 5 years.

If you expect to stay in your house at least five years, and if you can afford the higher monthly payments, you'll save tens of thousands of dollars in interest with a 15-year mortgage rather than one for 30 years. And you will own your home completely in half the time it takes with a 30-year loan.

ADVANTAGES

Advantages of a 15-year, fixed-rate loan include:
1. Monthly payments are fixed and predictable.
2. You'll get hefty interest savings over the life of the loan.
3. Rates can be 0.25 to 0.5 percentage point lower than on 30-year mortgages.
4. Equity in the home builds more quickly than with a 30-year loan.

DISADVANTAGES

You'll have to weigh at least two disadvantages:

1. Expect to make a larger monthly payment than on a 30-year loan. However, you may be surprised how little more it will be.
2. You'll need a larger annual income to qualify for the larger monthly payments; therefore you won't be able to purchase as expensive a home as you could with a 30-year loan.

FASTER PRINCIPAL PAYOFF

The 15-year loan is set up so that your home will be paid off in 180 equal monthly payments. The payment amount for principal and interest will remain the same over the course of the loan.

As with all mortgages, the majority of each payment is for interest for more than half of the loan's term. On a 15-year mortgage, however, a relatively substantial portion of the payment pays off the principal.

Relatively low interest rates prompt more homeowners to consider a 15-year, fixed-rate mortgage rather than the conventional 30-year mortgage.

In August 1985, the Mortgage Bankers Association of America reported that one in seven, or about 14 percent, of the home mortgages written for the previous 12 months were 15-year, fixed-rate loans.

"That figure is really substantial when you consider at the beginning of 1983 the percentage of 15-year loans across the country was practically zero," said Thomas O. Marder, an MBA spokesman.

Marder said 15-year mortgages began gaining popularity in 1984 when the interest rates dropped below 13 percent and borrowers realized how little the difference in payments is between 15-year and 30-year loans.

"People think their payments will double with the 15-year loan. But what they don't realize is most of their payments in the beginning of either loan go to pay interest and very little actually goes toward the principal," said Karl Reinlein, senior vice president and regional manager of GMAC Mortgage Corp. in St. Louis.

Although payments are higher on the 15-year mortgage, interest rates and points tend to be slightly less than on the 30-year loan. There is also faster equity buildup and quicker payoff of the loan. Middle-aged homeowners prefer 15-year mortgages because they have higher income and want their house to be paid off before retirement. Also, some ambitious young people who want to be rid of a mortgage quickly prefer to build up equity for their next home on the 15-year loan.

To determine equity growth, refer to the loan progress charts in the Appendix.

HOW INTEREST IS SAVED

Most of the savings on the 15-year mortgage comes from the accelerated repayment of the principal, though the lower interest rates help, too.

Because each month's interest is figured on the unpaid principal balance, every dollar paid on principal reduces the interest payment for the next month and every month after that. So, the extra payment toward principal of a 15-year loan lowers each month's interest portion of your payment, leaving more for principal. Clearly, this effect snowballs—in your favor.

When you compare monthly payments and total interest charges on a $100,000 mortgage for 30 and 15 years, the difference is dramatic.

Let's suppose your brother-in-law took out a 30-year loan at 10.75 percent. The monthly principal and interest payment would be $933.48.

If you borrowed the same amount for 15 years at 10.25 percent, the monthly payment would be $1,089.95. You would be paying $156.47 a month more than on the 30-year loan, but this entire amount would pay off the principal. You also benefit from having an interest rate that is 0.5 percentage point lower on the 15-year loan.

After five years of the 30-year loan, your brother-in-law would still owe $970 for every $1,000 borrowed, or $97,000 of the $100,000 loan. After 10 years, he would still owe $919 of every $1,000 borrowed, or $91,900.

Meanwhile, after five years of your 15-year loan, you'd owe $816 of every $1,000 you borrowed, or $81,600 of the $100,000 loan. However, after 10 years, you would owe only $510 of every $1,000 borrowed, or $51,000. After 15 years, you'd be hosting a mortgage-burning party, while your brother-in-law still would owe $83,300—*more than 83 percent of the original loan amount.* He would continue paying $11,201.78 each year for another 15 years.

But, your brother-in-law says, "I saved $156.47 every month." If he invested that difference and earned 7 percent, compounded annually, in 15 years it would grow to nearly $50,000. You'll save that much in the first five years after the mortgage-burning party, although inflation may reduce the value of this savings somewhat.

The following chart shows the monthly principal and interest payments for a 30-year and a 15-year fixed-rate mortgage for $75,000. You may be surprised at the

COMPARISON OF PAYMENTS

Comparison of Payments

Interest Rate	15-Year Loan	30-Year Loan
8.0%	$717.00	$550.50
8.5	738.75	576.75
9.0	761.25	603.75
9.5	783.75	630.75
10.0	806.25	658.50
10.5	829.50	686.25
11.0	852.75	714.75
11.5	876.75	743.25
12.0	900.75	771.75
12.5	924.75	801.00
13.0	949.50	830.25
13.5	974.25	859.50
14.0	999.00	888.75
14.5	1,024.50	918.75
15.0	1,050.00	948.75

difference. Also, remember that you often can obtain a lower interest rate on a 15-year loan than on a 30-year loan.

DRAWBACKS OF THE 15-YEAR MORTGAGE

While the 15-year loan is growing in popularity, it has some drawbacks.

Since the 15-year loan increases the amount of monthly payments, Reinlein pointed out that it limits the price range of a prospective home buyer.

"This loan is not for everyone because it definitely limits the amount of home you can buy," he said. "The typical person applying for a 15-year loan is someone who's owned a home before—someone who has a little discretionary income. It's not [usually] a loan for a newly married couple buying their first home. But it's a great loan and you build up equity fast. It just limits the amount of home you can buy."

The larger payments also are locked in, forcing you to pay that much. During hard times in the family budget, the larger payment may be a substantial drain. If you were voluntarily prepaying principal on a 30-year loan, however, you could stop doing so for a while without any problem.

CHAPTER 10

THE BIWEEKLY MORTGAGE

Biweekly Mortgage at a Glance

Interest rate: Lower than a 30-year mortgage and fixed for the life of the loan.
Rate adjustments: None.
Payment changes: None.
Term of loan: 15–19 years.
Maximum loan amount: $187,600, but lenders will make larger loans with slightly different terms.
Assumable: No.
Ideal for: Young professionals with high income.

The biweekly loan, nicknamed the "Yuppie mortgage," is a relatively new type of home financing that can save the borrower a lot in interest payments.

Under the biweekly plan, principal and interest

payments are set up as if the loan were for 30 years. But instead of paying once a month, you make one-half of the monthly payment every two weeks. Many borrowers find this more closely matches their paychecks anyway.

There are 26 payments each year—or the equivalent of 13 monthly payments every year rather than the usual 12. The extra money goes to pay down the principal of the loan—fast—and the process is relatively painless. Making what amounts to an extra payment a year may not sound like much of a change, but its effect in cutting the time and cost of any mortgage is astounding.

ADVANTAGES

The biweekly mortgage has three major advantages:

1. You get hefty savings on interest payments.
2. Equity builds up fast.
3. The mortgage principal is paid off at a rate almost twice that of a conventional 30-year mortgage.

DISADVANTAGES

Some disadvantages of biweekly mortgages include the following:

1. Mortgage payments are more frequent, and total yearly payments are larger than on 30-year loans.
2. Higher payments could lower the maximum loan amount if normal underwriting ratios are used.
3. You get smaller tax deductions for mortgage interest.
4. There are potential loan servicing problems.

HOW A BIWEEKLY MORTGAGE WORKS

The greater frequency of mortgage payments speeds up the loan payoff. That's because the portion of each payment that goes for interest is determined by the amount of unpaid principal. If you make payments every 14 days rather than every 30 or 31, the principal—and resulting interest charge—is lowered more quickly. The difference may be a dollar or two at first, but it grows quickly. Also, the equivalent of one extra monthly mortgage payment also reduces principal—and the following interest charges—dramatically.

IMPORTED FROM CANADA

The idea for making mortgage payments every two weeks began in Canada. Slowly it has made its way south, making the biggest inroads on the East Coast once its rate changed to fixed from the original adjustable.

Lenders tout the loan as a way to reduce the loan maturity period and overall interest expense by up to 40 percent.

This relatively new fixed-rate mortgage alternative has become popular with some young urban professionals—or yuppies—who live by electronic banking and credit cards. But it might fit blue-collar workers' cash flow even better. All told, nearly half of America's workers are paid biweekly, according to the Federal National Mortgage Association.

Even so, the biweekly mortgage has not become widely available or accepted, although it may be a chicken-or-egg situation. In Chicago, for example, the few lenders that offered biweekly loans in the late 1980s found they weren't as popular as expected. At Talman Home Mortgage Corp., biweekly loans accounted for only 15 percent of business in the first few months they were offered. "The response has not been bad, but it's not what I'd call overwhelming," said Executive Vice President Bob Brunner.

Other lenders just don't see the demand. Chicago-based Bell Federal Savings has studied the mortgage, but "frankly we don't see much of a market for it," said President Edmond Shanahan.

Whether or not more consumer awareness would lead to greater availability or the other way around, some experts still predict a promising future for the loan. They cite the growing acceptance of the 15-year, fixed-rate mortgage, which is being chosen by so many Americans that some lenders now consider it the "normal" fixed-rate mortgage.

Like a 15-year loan, the biweekly has higher annual payments, a shorter payoff period, and tens of thousands of dollars less in interest payments. The payment made every other week would be exactly half of the required monthly payment on a 30-year loan.

Challenges and Opportunities

There are both challenges and opportunities with the biweekly mortgage. On a typical biweekly mortgage, the borrower would make 495 biweekly payments, and the loan would be paid off in 19 years. The borrower would pay just over half the interest on a biweekly as over the course of a 30-year loan.

The 19-year payoff on the biweekly also results in rapid accumulation of net equity, and the borrower may pay a slightly lower interest rate and lower loan fees.

The biweekly payments also are a form of forced savings with tax-deferred capital gains, experts say. A young couple who buy a house with a biweekly mortgage, then have a family, will have equity on tap—ready to be borrowed just when their children reach college age.

A quick-payment mortgage also makes sense for middle-aged home buyers who want to own their house free and clear by the time they retire.

However, there are some disadvantages. The borrower may not like the increased total yearly payments required for housing—higher by 8.3 percent. The higher payments also will mean a family will qualify for a slightly smaller loan. Also, there will be less interest—less *deductible interest*—each year.

From a lender's viewpoint, servicing the loan is more complicated because there are 26 mortgage payments to collect and record each year, instead of 12. In the last few years, however, computer software has made that task easier, as have automatic withdrawals from a designated account with the lender. But whether the paperwork is done by a computer or a clerk, it still must be done—at a cost. Also, there may be an emotional hurdle for some borrowers who prefer to deal in cash or, at worst, checks, and want little to do with electronic funds transfers.

As an alternative, borrowers who are eager to reap the benefits of a quick-payoff mortgage can do so by paying extra each month toward their mortgage principal. An extra $50 or $100 paid each month will knock years off your mortgage and drastically reduce total interest charges. Just don't send it every two weeks unless the lender knows it's coming and is willing and able to process it. Principal prepayment will be discussed further in Chapter 17.

CHAPTER 11

FHA LOANS: HOW UNCLE SAM HELPS CASH-STRAPPED BORROWERS

> *FHA 203(B) Loan at a Glance*
>
> *Interest rate:* Fixed for the life of the loan. Sometimes lower than for conventional mortgages.
> *Rate adjustments:* None.
> *Payment changes:* None.
> *Term of loan:* 15 or 30 years.
> *Maximum loan amount:* up to $101,250, depending on location.
> *Assumable:* Yes.
> *Ideal for:* Young buyers with stable or slowly increasing income but relatively little savings.

The Federal Housing Administration (FHA) insures up to 20 percent of all home loans originated in the United States. These loans are extremely popular among young home buyers who are short on down payment cash but have solid monthly income.

FHA loans are particularly attractive because they require a lower minimum down payment. In addition, government-backed loans are fully assumable by a home's purchaser.

Since 1983, most of the paperwork for FHA loans has been shifted to the lenders involved and away from bureaucrats. This process known as direct endorsement has resulted in faster processing and fewer horror stories.

Unfortunately, some of the stories from several years ago still linger, leaving false impressions of FHA loans.

ADVANTAGES

FHA loans have a number of advantages:

1. Down payments are low. The minimum is 3 percent of the first $25,000 of *appraised value* plus 5 percent of the value over $25,000.
2. The loan is assumable by the home's next buyer.
3. Closing costs can be financed into the loan.

DISADVANTAGES

The negatives of FHA loans include the following:

1. High closing costs, a loan origination fee, and discount points are possible. Because interest rates on FHA loans usually are the lowest available in

the marketplace, lenders often charge higher points than for conventional loans to make their usual profit. However, points can be split by buyer and seller, and the purchaser can finance his or her share.
2. There is a maximum mortgage amount. Even in the most expensive areas of the country, the maximum is only $101,250, not enough for some would-be borrowers.
3. The insurance premium—usually financed at closing—is steep. It's 3.8 percent of the loan amount on 30-year loans and 2.4 percent on 15-year mortgages.

GOVERNMENT INSURANCE

The Federal Housing Administration provides government insurance for home loans. The FHA administers the insurance part of the programs, and mortgage bankers and other private lenders provide the money.

By insuring the loans, the FHA protects lenders and makes them more willing to lend to home buyers. Lenders are willing to lend to less-affluent borrowers if the federal government is helping to reduce the risk. But the borrower has to pay a price—either in a lump sum or monthly.

Most borrowers pay a one-time insurance premium of 3.8 percent of the 30-year loan amount or 2.4 percent of the 15-year sum. The FHA program allows borrowers to add this premium to their loan amount.

If the lender is qualified for the FHA coinsurance program—and this is less common—the government mortgage insurance premium is 0.5 percentage point added to the interest rate. So, a 10.25 percent FHA loan really becomes a 10.75 percent mortgage.

If you stay in the house a number of years, the two programs probably would cost you the same amount. If you plan to stay just a few years, avoid the one-time premium, from which you would receive a prorated refund after a few months of processing.

Before approving a loan, the FHA will appraise the house to determine its fair market value. It also will inspect the house to make sure it meets basic structural requirements. If a home doesn't measure up, the seller will have to make repairs and pay for them before the FHA gives the green light.

There are several types of FHA loans, including fixed-rate and graduated-payment loans, but the old-fashioned 30-year, fixed rate loan attracts the lion's share of borrowers. This chapter will focus on the fixed-rate FHA 203(B) loan. Graduated-payment loans will be covered in Chapter 15.

LOW DOWN PAYMENT

House hunters who qualify for an FHA-insured mortgage can buy a $60,000 home with a down payment of as little as $2,500, or 4.17 percent of the purchase price. (That's 3 percent of the first $25,000, or $750, plus 5 percent of the next $35,000, or $1,750, for a total of $2,500.)

The FHA 203(B) mortgage features a fixed, long-term interest rate. FHA rates no longer are set by the federal government—as they were until the early 1980s—but rise and fall depending on market conditions. The loans are available for 15 or 30 years. The interest rate on the 15-year variety generally is 0.25 to 0.5 percentage point less than on the 30-year loan, reflecting the smaller amount of interest-rate risk the lender has on a shorter mortgage.

CLOSING FEES

On FHA loans, borrowers also are required to pay a loan origination fee of 1 percent of the mortgage amount. Many other types of loans do not require such a fee. Then there's another 1 percent for such closing costs as title insurance premium, survey, title search, mortgage recording, and other fees.

While these are substantial expenses, an FHA loan—unlike most other loans—allows the buyer to finance most of the closing costs. Allowable closing costs include the loan origination fee, title insurance policy, escrow fees, recording fees, and credit report. But be careful; these items must be added to the sale price before calculating the maximum FHA loan amount.

So adding the fees to the loan amount reduces the cost of the home you can afford. And you will take 15 or 30 years to finally pay off the fees.

The mortgage insurance premium can be added to the mortgage amount, but it isn't considered in determining whether the loan fits under the maximum.

The FHA also allows the home seller and buyer to split "discount points" instead of forcing sellers to pay the whole amount and watch some of their profit go down the drain. Without the split, many sellers simply wouldn't sell to FHA borrowers.

In busy real estate markets, some sellers simply tack the points onto the price of the home or refuse to reduce the asking price for FHA borrowers while doing so for borrowers with conventional financing.

Discount points are special fees that lenders charge to increase their yield on these loans. A point equals 1 percent of the loan amount. Depending on market conditions, points can be from 1 percent to 8 percent of the loan amount, but most often they are in the range of 3 percent to 6 percent.

SETTING STANDARDS

To limit the risk and probability of foreclosure or collection difficulties, the FHA evaluates the financial background of applicants.

"We review the borrower's financial history to make sure he can meet the mortgage payments and still have enough cash left over to live a decent life," said David Podbelski, chief of mortgage credit at the Chicago office of the Department of Housing and Urban Development. After all, both the lender and the borrower lose out if a borrower is in over his or her head.

There are no maximum income limitations on FHA home loans; they are open to all who can qualify. A good credit history is one of the principal considerations, Podbelski said.

In applying for an FHA loan, a borrower must meet the following criteria, which are similar to other lenders' standards, though perhaps more lenient:

Good Credit History. FHA loan examiners depend heavily on information gathered by a reputable credit bureau about the borrower's previous record of financial responsibility.

"The loan examiner wants to know how the borrower manages his financial affairs," Podbelski said. "Uncle Sam believes past performance is the most reliable guide in determining the borrower's future credit behavior."

Usually at least two years of good credit history are required, unless the borrower is from a foreign country, has recently graduated from college or technical school, or has recently been discharged from military service. Unlike other lenders, however, FHA lenders will treat no credit as good credit.

Income Stability. Loan examiners look at employment information, an estimate of after-tax income, and details of financial obligations, such as credit card debt and other bills. The FHA credit examiner analyzes the borrower's income to determine whether it can be expected to continue through the first five years of the mortgage—the critical period during which most defaults occur. Only 24 months of employment are usually required.

Adequate Assets. Borrowers also must prove they have enough cash to cover the down payment and all closing costs, if they are not included in the mortgage amount.

In analyzing the borrower's credit record, Uncle Sam—like most lenders—does not blackball a borrower for an isolated case of unsatisfactory or slow payment of a debt or account. Instead, what counts is the general pattern of credit behavior.

CHAPTER 12

HOW VETERANS CAN BUY WITH LITTLE OR NO MONEY DOWN

> *VA Loan at a Glance*
>
> *Interest rate:* Maximum rate set by the Department of Veterans Affairs. Fixed rate for the life of the loan, usually slightly below market rates.
> *Rate adjustments:* None.
> *Payment changes:* None.
> *Term of loan:* 15 or 30 years.
> *Maximum loan guarantee:* $36,000. This means a veteran can buy a $144,000 house with no money down. For every $1,000 the veteran puts down, the mortgage limit rises by $4,000.
> *Assumable:* Yes.
> *Ideal for:* U.S. armed services veterans who are buying their first home and are short on down payment cash; veterans moving up to a larger home who want to take advantage of benefits they have earned.

Veterans of U.S. military service who want to buy a home haven't been forgotten by Uncle Sam or America's mortgage lenders.

Every year, nearly 200,000 veterans finance the purchase of houses—or refinance their homes—with mortgages guaranteed by the Department of Veterans Affairs. Since the loan guarantee program was launched in 1944 to help World War II veterans achieve the American dream of home ownership, the VA has backed 12.5 million mortgages. Through the program, veterans are allowed to buy homes with little or no down payment at a competitive interest rate.

In June 1989, when the federal government lowered the maximum interest rate on VA mortgages from 10.5 percent to 10 percent, this loan was one of the best home-financing deals available in the United States.

ADVANTAGES

Following are some advantages of VA loans:

1. VA loans require no money down or a small down payment.
2. Payments for principal and interest are predictable because the interest rate remains constant over the life of the loan.
3. The loan can be assumed by the home's next buyer. (If it is, the seller cannot take out another VA loan until this one is paid off.)
4. There is no prepayment penalty.

DISADVANTAGES

VA loans have a few disadvantages, too, including the following:

1. There are red tape and application delays, but not as bad as with FHA loans.
2. Because the government sets the interest rate, lenders may charge extra fees to bring the yield on the loan up to the level of other investments.

Like all fixed-rate loans, VA mortgages carry a fixed interest rate. So the mortgage payment for principal and interest remains the same each month for the life of the loan.

WHO IS ELIGIBLE FOR A VA LOAN?

Nearly 30 million veterans or their spouses are eligible for 15- and 30-year, fixed-rate VA-guaranteed mortgages that allow the purchase of a home with little or no money down. The borrower must be an honorably discharged military veteran with 181 days of service during wartime or generally two years during peacetime. Also eligible are unmarried surviving spouses of military personnel who died in service or from a service-related disability, and spouses of service members who have been captured or listed as missing in action.

Millions of veterans whose previous loans have been paid in full are eligible for new loans guaranteed by the Veterans Affairs Department. If a veteran sells a home purchased with a VA mortgage, he or she can get another VA loan once the first is paid off.

If a vet sells to another veteran who is eligible, the purchaser's entitlement can be transferred to the seller. The seller then may buy another house using the buyer's entitlement.

Also, if a veteran still has partial eligibility, he or she may buy a second home without selling the first one. Specifics about partial eligibility are available from the Veterans Administration.

A vet who sells his or her house and lets the loan be assumed by another borrower must obtain a release of liability from the VA loan-processing section. Otherwise, if the new borrower defaults, the vet can be held liable for whatever loss the VA suffers because it has to meet a claim under the guarantee.

TERMS OF A VA LOAN

Under current VA loan guarantees, eligible veterans have a $36,000 housing entitlement, which means they can borrow up to $144,000 for the purchase of a single-family home or a two- to four-unit apartment building with no money down.

The $36,000 in loan guarantee gives lenders risk protection on 25 percent of a loan. Therefore, a veteran can borrow up to four times that amount, or $144,000. However, veterans who make a down payment can get a VA loan for a house costing more than $144,000, said Alan Schneider, VA loan guarantee officer for Illinois.

Let's say you make a $10,000 down payment. Add that to the $36,000 in VA guarantee. Then multiply $46,000 by 4, and your mortgage limit becomes $184,000.

Of course, VA borrowers face the usual credit evaluation and must be able to repay the loan. They also must live in the building being financed.

Vets also can use a VA loan to finance the purchase of a condominium or a mobile home, with or without a lot. The funding can be used to construct, rehab, repair, or refinance a home.

Veteran buyers can buy an apartment building with other vets and develop their own co-op housing. They can use part of the loan to pay for their own labor and materials to upgrade their living units.

VA LOAN FEES

Veterans must pay a loan origination fee of 1 percent of the mortgage amount. Closing costs are 1 percent for title insurance premium, survey, title search, mortgage recording, and other fees. The VA also charges a 1 percent loan guarantee fee, which can be added to the mortgage amount. This money is funneled into the VA loan guarantee fund to help make the program more self-sufficient. This revolving fund is used to pay off lenders' claims resulting from foreclosure.

So, the buyer pays a total of three points on a typical VA loan.

Critics of the VA no-down-payment provision say it encourages irresponsible buyers to walk away from a home when finances become too much, leaving Uncle Sam to help pay off the lender and depleting loan guarantee resources. That's why experts are proposing the Veterans' Home Loan Indemnity Act as an alternative to the revolving fund. The act would increase the funding fee to 1.25 percent for no-down-payment VA loans, and decrease it to 0.75 percent for loans with at least 5 percent down.

Because the VA loan rate is set by Uncle Sam and usually is slightly below market rates, lenders charge points ranging from 2 to 6 percent of the loan amount to increase their yield. Under VA regulations, these points must be paid by the seller and not packed into the price of the house.

Sometimes, however, it's hard to ensure that this is true. After all, why would the seller want to lose 6 percent of his or her profit by selling to a VA borrower rather than a conventional borrower?

If you are a veteran who has not taken advantage of your VA-guaranteed loan benefits, check with your local VA office for details, or contact the Veterans Administration, Washington, D.C. 20420.

CHAPTER 13

MORTGAGE BOND FINANCING: POPULAR AND ENDANGERED

Mortgage Bond Loans at a Glance

Interest rate: Usually 2 or 3 percentage points below market rates.
Rate adjustment: None.
Payment changes: None.
Term of loan: 30 years.
Mortgage amount: Any amount for homes costing up to 10 percent above the median-priced home in the local community.
Assumable: No.
Ideal for: First-time home buyers.

In the last decade and a half, 49 states have issued billions of dollars' worth of tax-exempt bonds to make fixed-rate home loans available for first-time buyers at below-market rates. In the 50th state, Kansas, local governments issue bonds.

Under these programs, families with annual incomes as low as $20,000 can purchase new or resale homes. Usually rates are 2 or 3 percentage points lower than the conventional mortgage rate, depending on the bond market.

ADVANTAGES

Among the advantages of mortgage bond financing are the following:

1. Interest rates are substantially below market rates.
2. Down payment requirements are low.
3. Borrower income requirements are easier to meet.
4. Rates and payments for principal and interest are fixed for the length of the mortgage.

DISADVANTAGES

There are two main disadvantages:

1. Only first-time buyers—and sometimes other buyers in depressed areas—are eligible.
2. Because of heavy demand, these loans often are distributed by lottery. So, borrowers often have to be both needy and lucky.

HOW ONE BOND PLAN WORKS

While fixed mortgage rates hovered around 10.75 percent in early 1989, 3,000 to 3,500 first-time home buyers in Illinois obtained 30-year fixed-rate loans at 8.58 percent through a state mortgage bond plan.

Instead of using a lottery as it had in previous years,

the Illinois Housing Development Authority distributed the $200 million in loans through 52 lenders and 30 home builders on a first-come, first-served basis. The lottery's paperwork had slowed down the process unnecessarily and sellers often weren't willing to wait to see if buyers would win a loan and then wait for it to be processed, said Peter Dwars, the authority's director.

Within weeks, all of the funds available for resale homes had been spoken for. It didn't take much longer for new-home buyers to use up their share.

To qualify, a family in the Chicago area couldn't make more than $44,620 to $53,245, depending on the specific location. Nor could a new single-family home cost more than $106,920 to $178,830 or a resale home $69,300 to $121,590. There also were maximum purchase prices for two- to four-unit apartments.

Tax-exempt bond financing cannot be used for homes costing more than 10 percent above the median-priced home in the local community. Also, at least 20 percent of the money raised through the bond sale must be used in economically distressed neighborhoods.

Illinois also required that the borrower hadn't owned a home in the previous three years—its definition of a first-time buyer. Borrowers also had to pay a loan origination fee of 1 percent of the loan amount.

Since 1982, the Illinois Housing Development Authority had made 17,000 loans to first-time home buyers, financing $1 billion in home loans.

WHY MORTGAGE BOND RATES ARE LOWER

The money for these programs is raised by selling bonds to investors. The bonds meet U.S. requirements that make the interest paid to the investors free from federal income taxes. Because investors don't lose a substantial portion of their interest income to Uncle Sam, they are willing to accept a lower interest rate. The lower interest rate is then passed along to borrowers.

U.S. TREASURY OPPOSITION

Despite the popularity of these programs with borrowers, state and local governments, and the housing industry, this type of financing has come under fire from the federal government, desperate to reduce the deficit.

The Reagan administration worried about the loss of federal revenue, assuming that without the tax-free bonds, investors would choose bonds on which the government could tax the interest. In 1981 and 1982—two of the biggest years for tax-exempt mortgage revenue bonds since states began participating in 1970—the financing programs cost the federal government more than $2.6 billion in lost revenue, according to the Government Accounting Office.

For that reason, Congress has restricted use of the program to single-family homes for first-time buyers and placed a cap on the volume of bonds a state and all of its localities may issue.

In the late 1980s, Congress extended the program a year at a time. It wasn't until late in 1988, for example, that states knew that they could offer loans in 1989. These short-term extensions frustrated program administrators, who found planning, timing, and staffing much more difficult to handle.

Also in 1988, a new wrinkle was proposed. Apparently concerned that first-time buyers were getting rich on homes bought with bargain-interest loans, some bureaucrats suggested that borrowers pay back part of the rate discount if they sell the home within 10 years. Though that portion of the proposal failed to pass Congress in 1988, it reappeared in 1989 and could be part of the package that could extend the program for three years.

No formula has been devised for figuring this payback, and program administrators are concerned that this will scare away moderate-income, first-time buyers, who are relatively less sophisticated than move-up buyers.

Curtailing or restricting the program would hurt moderate-income home buyers.

Without a program aiding families who cannot afford conventional mortgage rates, "there is no way you're going to get those people into houses," said Robert Sonneck of the Minnesota Housing Finance Agency. "We're not in business to compete with banks. Because of the tax exemption, we can provide a product banks cannot provide."

CHAPTER 14

ADJUSTABLE-RATE MORTGAGES: A CHANGE IN THE RULES

> ### *ARMs at a Glance*
>
> *Interest rate:* Initially about 2 percentage points lower than a conventional fixed-rate loan; in the second period may be comparable to a fixed-rate mortgage.
> *Rate adjustment:* Usually every one, three, or five years, depending on the mortgage. Most loans limit how much the rate can change each period and over the length of the loan.
> *Payment changes:* Can change as often as rates can—every one, three, or five years.
> *Term of loan:* 30 years.
> *Assumable:* Yes.
> *Ideal for:* White-collar workers who expect to be transferred within three years and other borrowers who have the financial means to handle increased payments, but expect interest rates to decline.

Mortgage lenders love adjustable-rate home loans. That's probably the biggest reason home buyers should be wary of them, consumer advocates say.

Getting a handle on how much a home buyer will pay over the life of an adjustable-rate mortgage (ARM) is like trying to grab hold of an eel. And the unwary borrower who chooses an ARM may feel wrapped in the embrace of an octopus. Eventually the borrower may be swimming in a sea of red ink.

ADVANTAGES

ARMs do have advantages. Following are the three major ones:

1. Below-market, first-year payments make the first year (period) of home ownership easier to adjust to financially.
2. Consumers are protected by annual and life-of-loan caps on rate and payments.
3. Borrowers can benefit from future interest-rate declines without the costs and hassles of refinancing.

DISADVANTAGES

In terms of disadvantages, you'll want to consider the following:

1. Rate and payment increases in second and subsequent years (periods) can shock the borrower's budget.
2. Negative amortization is possible.
3. The future cost of a home is impossible to know.

HOW ARMs WORK

ARMs allow lenders to change the borrower's interest rate, monthly payment, and/or principal balance based on shifts in economic indicators, or indexes. Lenders adjust the interest rate on the loan in regular prespecified intervals—usually every one, three, or five years—based on movements of the index. Lenders then add a profit margin of 2 to 3 percentage points to compute the new rate.

Typical indexes on which ARMs are adjusted include the one-year T-bill index, an average of U.S. securities yields, or the Federal Home Loan Bank Board's national or regional cost-of-funds indexes, which chart the average rates federally chartered S&Ls pay savers and other lenders.

Most banks and S&Ls would prefer borrowers to choose ARMs because the flexible rate protects the institution in times of inflation. Instead of being locked into fixed-rate obligations—as many S&Ls and banks were in the early 1980s—the financial institution can pass along to borrowers rate increases allowed under terms of the loan. This leaves the borrower, not the lender, at the mercy of rate charges.

A BAD REPUTATION

Adjustable mortgages got a bad reputation in the early 1980s when rates were high and still-evolving ARMs were the only type of financing many people could afford.

In 1983 and 1984, when fixed-rate loans were above 13 percent, it was not uncommon for lenders to quote a first-year ARM rate as low as 6 or 7 percent. Despite the first-year bargains, ARM borrowers found themselves paying close to the same rate as on fixed mortgages when the loans were adjusted for the second year. And the mortgage agreement allowed the rate to go even higher if the index of rates did.

More recently, however, interest-rate and payment caps were added to protect borrowers. Even so, the amount of the monthly check the borrower sends the lender can change annually or every three or five years. That doesn't sit well with many borrowers.

In 1984 nearly two-thirds of the home-loan origination activity was in ARMs, compared to only 5 percent in 1981. However, in 1985, the share of ARM loan activity dropped to about 50 percent. With the decline of mortgage rates and the re-emergence of affordable fixed-rate loan alternatives, experts say ARMs lost momentum, but they probably will be a fixture in the future marketplace.

"Its share of the market may rise and fall depending on market interest rates, but the ARM has become a permanent feature of the mortgage market," said John B. Zellars, former chairman of the U.S. League of Savings Institutions, a trade organization that represents the S&L industry.

Lenders also say ARMs keep mortgage money available during times of high interest rates. When interest rates—especially long-term fixed rates—rose in mid-1982, ARMs were available to borrowers. Few buyers would have—or could have—taken on fixed-rate loans at 15 percent.

A FLUCTUATING MARKET

The share of the mortgage market that goes to ARMs usually depends on interest rates. First, what's the going charge on fixed-rate loans? Second, what's the difference between that and the starting rate on an ARM?

During 1986, for example, when rates dropped briefly to near 9 percent on 30-year fixed loans, lenders that concentrated on ARMs had trouble generating large volume. Borrowers wisely locked in those rates, which did not reappear during the rest of the decade.

As the decade went on and fixed rates rose, ARMs staged a comeback. Borrowers looking to spend as little as possible in the early years of a mortgage signed on for initial rates that sometimes were more than 2.5 percentage points lower than those on fixed loans. For borrowers who moved within a few years, the situation was ideal.

In 1989, however, short-term rates on which ARMs are based rose sharply, relative to long-term rates. That cut the difference between ARMs and fixed loans to 1.5 percentage points in some cases. With such little incentive for ARMs, borrowers wary of future increases opted for fixed loans.

Another factor at work was the waning of artificially low initial rates that lure a borrower in, only to boomerang in future years. With more realistic starting rates, borrowers have a clearer idea of what the costs could be.

Still, home buyers must be cautious. If a loan's rate rises the maximum 2 percentage points a year for two or three years, the American dream of home ownership and a borrower's good credit history could be obliterated by red ink.

STANDARDIZED ARM REQUIREMENTS

Today, fewer ARMs are like icebergs, hiding many vices. Without ridiculously low teaser rates, fewer consumers will be caught unprepared by the shifting tide of payments.

The seeds of this change were sown in mid-1984,

when Congress pressured the mortgage industry to standardize ARMs. Today, some general requirements apply. (The first five requirements are no different from those used for 30-year, fixed-rate loans.) These requirements are:

1. A borrower's first-year mortgage payment usually must be no more than 28 percent of his or her gross income.
2. The maximum loan amount generally is $187,600, though some savings and loans will lend as much as $500,000.
3. Monthly payments are based on a 30-year amortization schedule.
4. The minimum down payment is 5 percent, but most lenders now require 10 percent down.
5. If the down payment is less than 20 percent, private mortgage insurance will be required to protect the lender from default.
6. Generally, movements in the interest rates on capped adjustable mortgages are limited to 2 percentage points per year and 5 or 6 percentage points over the life of the loan.
7. Adjustable programs will limit negative amortization to 125 percent of the mortgage amount. (Negative amortization occurs if the interest rate on an ARM is adjusted upward and monthly payments do not cover interest charges. The interest owed is tacked onto the loan amount.)

ARM PLANS VARY

There are several ARM plans approved by the Federal National Mortgage Association and available at S&Ls, banks, and mortgage companies.

The most popular ARM program calls for annual interest-rate and payment adjustments. In the late 1980s, depending on the lender originating the mortgage, most first-year interest rates ranged from 8 percent to 10 percent. Lenders generally charge points, or closing costs, of 2 percent to 3 percent of the loan amount.

Although this plan currently is the most viable ARM program, borrowers should shop for the best rates at S&Ls eager to peddle this loan. Be sure to ask the lender what index is used and what margin is added. Have the lender compute the second- and third-year rate and payment based on today's index and the margin.

ARM SCENARIOS

One-Year ARM

Suppose you need a $90,000 home loan and take out a typical one-year ARM from your local savings and loan association. With a first-year rate of 8.5 percent amortized over 30 years, monthly principal and interest payments would be $692.

You'd also have to pay the usual closing costs, including three points—$2,700—and a $250 loan application fee. With a minimum down payment of 10 percent, private mortgage insurance would be required. There would be a first-year insurance premium of 0.4 percent of the loan amount—$360.

The second-year insurance fee would be 0.34 percent of the loan balance, or about $300 a year. Payable in monthly installments, that would increase your monthly payment to about $717.

Suppose future interest-rate adjustments are based on the Federal Home Loan Bank Board's national cost-of-funds index. Then, a 2.5 percentage-point margin for costs and profit is added to the index value.

If the index were at 9 percent after one year, the second-year rate on your ARM would be 11.5 percent (9 percent plus the 2.5 percentage-point margin). Your principal and interest payments would rise to about $891. The PMI would raise your total monthly payment to about $916 from $717. That's a payment jump of nearly 28 percent in the second year.

The payment cap of 2 percentage points, however, would limit the rate to 10.5 percent in the second year. Even so, the new payment for mortgage and PMI would be $848, an increase of 18.3 percent.

A number of lenders will allow borrowers to set a *payment cap*, usually of 7.5 percent. In those cases, however, negative amortization occurs when the difference between the payment and what should have been paid is added to the mortgage balance.

Three-Year and Five-Year ARMs

A three-year or five-year ARM is a hybrid, providing the certainty of fixed rates and payments, but only for three or five years. Like ARMs and fixed loans, these hybrids are figured to pay off the loan amount in 30 years.

The rates on such loans generally fall between the starting rate on an annually adjusted mortgage and that on a 30-year fixed loan. In 1989, for example, one lender was charging 8.375 percent on the first year of a one-year ARM, 9.75 percent for the first three years of a three-year ARM, and 10.25 percent for the first five years of a five-year ARM. The going rate on a 30-year, fixed loan was 10.75 percent.

There are several variations on three- and five-year ARMs, so make sure you ask lots of questions.

Some lenders lock in the rate and payments for the initial period but change them *annually* starting in year 4 or 6. Others will change the rate after the initial period but lock in for another three or five years. It makes a big difference.

Still another variation is for the payments to remain constant for the period, but for the rate to change, opening the door to negative amortization.

Like one-year ARMs, three- and five-year ARMs usually carry rate caps. They also are adjusted based on indexes, but be sure to ask which index will be used.

These hybrid ARMs will satisfy borrowers who are looking for fixed payments but don't want to pay the going rate for 30-year, fixed loans.

ARMs CAN BE CONVERTED

Many adjustable plans allow the borrower the option of converting an ARM to a fixed-rate loan at a specified time, usually the anniversary of the closing. This option was added to attract borrowers who wanted a fixed rate but couldn't afford it at the time the loan was made.

However, Michael L. Allen, president of Crown Mortgage Company in Oak Lawn, Illinois, advises borrowers to ask about the program's conversion factor.

If a borrower wants to convert to a fixed loan, some lenders will do so at the current market rate for fixed-rate loans plus a margin, usually 0.25 percentage point. The ARM rate—either current or when you took the loan—has nothing to do with the fixed interest rate at conversion.

In addition, there may be stipulated conversion costs, and you may have to pay a higher rate on the ARM for the conversion option.

Despite vast improvements in ARMs to increase consumer protection, to many borrowers these lending programs—with their caps, indexes, and margins—are still about as clear as octopus ink. But lenders continue to tout ARMs as the greatest invention since the life preserver.

CHAPTER 15
GRADUATED-PAYMENT LOANS AND OTHER INNOVATIVE MORTGAGES

GPM Loans at a Glance

Interest rate: Rate is fixed for entire length of the loan.
Rate adjustment: None.
Payment changes: Monthly payments start out low, increase gradually over the first five or ten years of the loan, then level off. Payments usually are larger than on a normal fixed-rate loan in the remaining years of the mortgage to repay the shortfall (negative amortization) in the early years.
Term of loan: 15 to 30 years.
Assumable: No.
Ideal for: Young buyers who expect their income to increase steadily over the years.

The graduated-payment mortgage (GPM) is designed primarily for young buyers on the way up—those who expect their income to increase steadily over the years. The loan is ideal for those who cannot afford higher payments now but whose potential indicates a higher income level in the near future.

The idea behind the GPM is to provide smaller-than-normal payments in the early years of the loan and larger-than-normal payments in the later years. Regulations regarding the GPM were incorporated into the National Housing Act of 1974. In 1977, the Federal Housing Administration introduced the FHA 245 program, a GPM loan that helped countless thousands of young buyers afford homes.

Monthly payments on a GPM start out lower than they would under a fixed-payment mortgage, but they will surpass a similar fixed-rate loan when they level off in five to ten years.

Buyers opting for a GPM may choose from a varied menu of payment schedules. For example, for the first five years, payments could increase 2.5 percent, 5 percent, or 7.5 percent annually, then level off for the remaining years of the loan. Another option is annual payment increases of 2 percent for 10 years, then level payments until the loan is paid off.

A new GPM plan—the 15-year Homeowner's Key loan—introduced by Citicorp Savings of Illinois, requires interest-only payments in the first year and small amounts of principal repayment in the next few years. In this example, the fixed-rate GPM loan carries an interest rate of 10.75 percent. However, the first-year payments are based on a rate of only 5.75 percent. The monthly payment increases each year by 7.5 percent until it reaches a level payment in year 8.

To avoid negative amortization, the borrower pays 0.789 percent of the loan amount into an interest-bear-ing subsidiary account at closing. Because the first-year payments will not cover the interest due, money will be drawn monthly from the subsidy account to cover the difference. There is no negative amortization, so the borrower's principal balance never will increase.

By the end of the second year, the 7.5 percent increase in monthly payment more than covers the interest due, and the subsidy account will be depleted. The monthly payments gradually continue to increase in years 3 through 7. The payments level off in years 8 through 15.

An extraordinarily serious drawback of the GPM is financial hardship and possible loss of the home if a borrower's income has not kept pace as expected.

A second drawback to the GPM is negative amortization. Because the payments in the early years are less than the interest owed, the monthly shortfall is added to the unpaid balance.

You'll pay a great deal more interest on a GPM than on a similar conventional fixed-rate mortgage. You'll get a tax deduction, but for a person in the 28 percent tax bracket, the additional tax deductions are worth only 28 cents on the dollar.

If you sell your house after six or seven years, you'll owe more money than you did when you first took out the loan. This gives you less equity for purchasing another home.

GROWING-EQUITY MORTGAGE

Growing-equity mortgages are geared for borrowers who expect their income to increase substantially within a few years. On these loans, the monthly payments will increase annually to pay off the loan faster.

> ### GEM Loans at a Glance
>
> *Interest rate:* Rate is fixed for entire length of the loan.
> *Rate adjustment:* None.
> *Payment changes:* In years 2 through 6, the monthly payment may increase annually, then level off.
> *Term of loan:* 13 to 17 years.
> *Assumable:* No.
> *Ideal for:* Upwardly mobile borrowers who expect their income to increase much faster than inflation.

Much like a 15-year, fixed-rate mortgage, the GEM is based on larger payments than on 30-year loans, faster equity growth, and a shorter mortgage term.

ADVANTAGES

The pluses to consider with the GEM are the following:

1. Equity grows rapidly through gradually increasing principal payments.
2. Total interest payments are less than on 30-year, fixed-rate loans.
3. The first-year payment is below the market rate.

DISADVANTAGES

The minuses to consider are the following:

1. After the first year, payments generally are higher than on a 15-year fixed loan.

2. If income doesn't keep pace with rising monthly payments, the cost of home ownership may be prohibitive.

RISING INCOME NEEDED

Typically, monthly payments rise slightly each year—by 3 or 4 percent—with all the increased cash flow paying off the outstanding principal and giving the borrower more equity in the home. At the same time, the higher payments help decrease the length of the loan.

Lenders like GEMs because they collect the borrower's interest and principal payments faster through the accelerated cash flow and can reinvest them. This provides the lender more protection against inflation.

There are many variations on the GEM theme, but only two basic plans. One starts out with a rate and payments much like a 30-year, fixed-rate mortgage, but the payments increase annually until the loan is paid off. The extra amount goes entirely toward principal, and the loan usually is paid off in 13 to 17 years. This choice is preferable for borrowers because they never lose equity.

Another widely used GEM involves artificially low payments in the early years, which cause the loan's principal balance to *increase* for a few years through negative amortization. Payments increase annually until year 6, when they level off. The increase in payments goes toward principal, helping to retire the loan early.

Only borrowers who are unable to make the necessary payments for the first variation of a GEM should look at this second choice. That's because there is negative amortization and the annual percentage rate on this loan usually is higher than on a fixed-rate, level-payment, 15-year mortgage—a plan the GEM attempts to mimic.

Here's how this GEM would work. Let's assume the first-year monthly payment is based on an interest rate of 9.5 percent. In years 2 through 6, the monthly payment increases 7.5 percent. The rate on which the payment is based increases by 1 percentage point annually, leveling off at 14.5 percent and remaining there for the rest of the 15-year loan.

The annual percentage rate averages 13.78 percent over the life of the loan. That's a terrible deal, considering that today you can lock in a 15-year, fixed-rate loan for a much, much lower rate. Also, because early-year payments are artificially low, a borrower will owe more upon sale after three years than at the original closing.

The maximum loan amount under a GEM ranges from $187,600 to $300,000, and down payments run from 5 percent to 20 percent. Lenders also charge points and a loan application fee. If the down payment is less than 20 percent, private mortgage insurance is required.

SHARED-APPRECIATION MORTGAGE

With a shared-appreciation mortgage (SAM), the buyer gets a lower interest rate by agreeing to share part of the increased value of the property with the lender when the house is sold.

Typically, the lender would offer an interest rate about one-third lower than the prevailing market rate and in return receive one-third of the owner's appreci-

> ### SAM Loans at a Glance
>
> *Interest rate:* The rate can be significantly lower than conventional fixed mortgages. However, the borrower must share with the lender the home's increased value when the loan term expires or the house is sold.
> *Rate adjustment:* None.
> *Payment changes:* Monthly payments are fixed for the life of the loan.
> *Term of loan:* 10 years.
> *Assumable:* No.
> *Ideal for:* Borrowers with potential for higher income who want to buy a more expensive home now, but can't qualify for the monthly payments.

ation when the home is sold. In effect, the lender becomes the homeowner's partner.

Let's suppose the going rate on a 30-year, fixed mortgage is 15 percent, and you need a $90,000 loan. Monthly principal and interest payments would be $1,138. But the lender offers you a SAM loan at 10 percent—and a monthly payment of $790. You save $348 a month, or $4,176 a year.

Seven years later, your $100,000 house is worth $142,000. One-third of that appreciation—$14,000—goes to the lender. It won't be fun writing that check.

And if you don't want to sell after 10 years, the usual length of a SAM, you may have to get the home appraised, pay the lender his or her share, and refinance the expired mortgage.

In addition, there are tax implications. You can deduct the lender's share of any appreciation from your federal income tax as interest. Your share of the appreciation would be a capital gain.

Consumer groups have other concerns about SAMs. Who pays for improvements to the home? Should the lender pay one-third the cost of a room addition or a new roof? How about the homeowner's labor for maintaining the property?

Because interest rates are low and other mortgage financing is available, these questions are currently moot. Except during times of relatively high interest rates, no wise borrower will touch a SAM.

CHAPTER 16

MORTGAGES FOR THE ELDERLY

> ### Grannie Maes at a Glance
>
> *Interest rate:* Yield based on return on annuity.
> *Rate adjustment:* None.
> *Payment changes:* None.
> *Term of loan:* Depends on age of borrower.
> *Assumable:* No.
> *Ideal for:* Elderly borrowers who want to convert the equity in their house into cash but don't want to move.

Being house-rich and cash-poor is a dilemma for many of America's nearly 20 million elderly homeowners. Because a person's house is also his or her home, the elderly person often thinks of that asset as untouchable.

But the relatively golden retirement annuity mortgage, or "Grannie Mae," may be the pot of gold about which every retiree dreams.

ADVANTAGES

Some advantages of the Grannie Mae are these:

1. It allows an elderly homeowner to convert home equity into cash without being forced to move.
2. The borrower is guaranteed a life-long lease.
3. The investor gets a tax break by writing off maintenance, repairs, and depreciation on the income property.

DISADVANTAGES

The homeowner should consider at least three disadvantages:

1. The elderly homeowner must find an investor willing and financially able to handle the commitment.
2. The fair market rent may be too high for the borrower to pay.
3. Closing costs are higher than for a conventional loan.

SOLVING THE CASH FLOW PROBLEM

Grannie Mae involves the sale of a home to the owner's child or children. The buyer then rents the home back at fair market value. In addition, the parent receives a lifetime lease on the home and a monthly payment—for life—that is funded by the home's selling price.

Because the Grannie Mae requires the sale of the property to a child or group of children, the lender never is the landlord, nor can the lender ever evict the elderly resident. Instead, the lender's involvement is limited to issuing a mortgage for the child/investor. Even if the children sell the home or the lender is forced to foreclose, the parent's lease continues.

The child or children get a tax break by writing off maintenance, repairs, and depreciation on the income property—expenses that wouldn't be deductible if the parent owned the home.

Often the home-buying child is in a higher tax bracket than the retired parent, so deductions for mortgage interest, property taxes, and other costs are more advantageous to the younger generation. The higher the child/investor's income tax bracket, the better the Grannie Mae works.

Annuity Pays the Rent

The monthly payment or annuity, resulting from the investment of the sale proceeds with an insurance company, pays the rent directly to the child/investor. Any amount more than the rent is paid directly to the elderly person for the rest of his or her life.

The annuity payment could be structured to increase at a predetermined rate every year to cover anticipated increases in rental costs—and to represent compounding of the principal amount.

Of course, an annuity payment that does not change will start out much higher than one that will increase. The amount of the annuity is based on the investment and the age and sex of the elderly resident(s).

An annuity for a 55-year-old man is structured to pay out for 22 years, the person's life expectancy. For a 55-year-old woman, it will pay out for 26 years. And for a 55-year-old couple, it will pay out for 30 years.

In contrast, the annuity is structured for just 6 years for an 85-year-old man, 8 years for an 85-year-old woman, and 9 years for an 85-year-old couple. Each payment would be larger for an 85-year-old than a 55-year-old.

If a 55-year-old man dies at 57, the balance is remitted to the estate. If, however, he lives until age 85, he will have received monthly payments for 30 years.

To see how Grannie Mae works, let's take the example of a $100,000 home sold to a child/investor by a 55-year-old widower. On the $100,000, there would be $4,200 in loan origination fees, and title insurance and closing costs would have to be paid, leaving $95,800 to invest in the annuity.

The selling widower would receive a monthly annuity of $772 for the rest of his life. In turn, the widower would pay $500 a month for rent and still have $272 from the home for other expenses. Of course, any pension and Social Security income would be additional.

There Are Drawbacks

Financial planners warn that, as with most innovative mortgages, Grannie Mae has disadvantages and may not be for everyone. Here are a few of the sticking points:

Negative Cash Flow for the Child/Investor. Although the child/investor receives the tax advantages of owning an investment property, the rental payments seldom cover the mortgage payments. That means such a plan requires monthly cash outlay.

Parental Allowance. Even with the annuity payment, pension, and Social Security, the parents may not have enough money for other living costs after paying a fair market rent. Supportive children may have to give money to their parents to help make ends meet.

Sibling Partnerships. If more than one child/investor owns the house, various siblings may have different financial resources and different needs. What happens if the roof has to be replaced or if one child/investor needs cash for immediate expenses several years into a Grannie Mae?

Tax Liability. What happens if the parent dies and the child/investors haven't finished paying off the Grannie Mae? Such possibilities should be addressed in the parent's will. This is one excellent reason to use an attorney at the closing of the Grannie Mae.

Costly Fees. There is also a fee for the Grannie Mae. Some lenders charge up to 4 percent of the loan amount in closing costs. Using the standardized Grannie Mae documents reduces the usual legal costs of setting up such a financial arrangement, but an attorney should be consulted before anything is signed. After all, you can be sure the lender's attorneys have everything in the contract that *they* want.

The idea for Grannie Mae was developed by Kenneth Rosen, chairman of the real estate program at the University of California at Berkeley. Today, these loans are being offered by the Family Backed Mortgage Association, a for-profit group.

"With the Grannie Mae, an elderly person is not

taking his total equity and gambling it away," said Richard Puntillo, president of Family Backed Mortgage Association.

Although Grannie Mae loans are relatively rare, Puntillo said, the mortgage has 12 million to 15 million potential clients. "It's a new concept," he explained. "It takes time to convince people that it's doable and in their best interests."

REVERSE EQUITY MORTGAGES

With the reverse equity mortgage (REM), there is no need for a family member to act as investor. The lender enters into an agreement with a homeowner regarding the equity in his or her home.

REMs at a Glance

Interest rate: Yield is based on rate set by lender.
Rate adjustment: None.
Payment changes: None.
Term of Loan: 10 years to lifetime.
Assumable: No.
Ideal for: Elderly persons who want to convert the equity in their house into cash, but don't want to move.

Such programs are possible only for homeowners who have a very small mortgage or none at all. The theory behind the reverse equity mortgage is that elderly homeowners would use up some or all of their home's equity while they are alive and thus be able to live more independently.

The concept was introduced in 1981 when the Federal Home Loan Bank Board authorized the nation's savings and loan associations to write them on an experimental basis. However, only a few S&Ls have done so.

Since then, these mortgages have been discussed widely but made rarely. They have been available in small numbers in some markets and not available at all in many other areas. In the late 1980s, however, that began to change, ever so slowly.

FHA Pilot Program

In 1987, Congress authorized the Federal Housing Administration to insure 2,500 reverse equity loans across the country in a pilot program. Although FHA usually tests loan programs with a much larger number of loans, advocates cheered any steps forward for cash-strapped elderly homeowners. The FHA insurance makes the loans attractive to lenders, who now see a chance to serve customers at a reduced risk.

When FHA finally ironed out the details and got serious about the program in 1989, a lottery was held to select 50 lenders who each could make 50 reverse mortgages. Each had a state or several states to serve.

A total of 258 lenders had applied, and FHA had a waiting list in every region, said Judith V. May, a policy analyst for the Department of Housing and Urban Development in Washington, D.C. The evaluation of the results by the lenders and FHA will determine whether the program will be expanded.

"The interest [from borrowers] has extended all the way across the country," May said. "I've received dozens of calls from Iowa. Before FHA got involved, the products were available in limited parts of the country with high appreciation, such as Connecticut, Rhode Island, and California."

The FHA program is likely to set the standard for reverse equity mortgages nationwide. The homeowner takes out a loan or line of credit and pledges his or her home as collateral. As the owed interest accumulates or additional money is borrowed, the loan balance contines to grow each month. Because interest is accruing and compounding at the same time, the loan balance will grow quickly.

Unlike home equity loans, however, no repayment is required until the term of the loan expires, which may be at a set time or when the owner moves out. When the home is sold, the proceeds from its sale pay off the loan.

The FHA pilot program allows elderly homeowners three ways to tap into their equity:

1. *Tenure option*—The homeowner receives a monthly payment as long as he or she occupies the house. This payout mimics the Grannie Mae mortgages described earlier in this chapter.
2. *Term option*—The homeowner can receive monthly payments for a period of time of his or her choosing. Of course, the longer the period, the smaller the payment.
3. *Line-of-credit option*—The homeowner can take money as needed, up to a specified maximum. A variation of this option is a one-time, lump-sum payment.

FHA limits the maximum amount of equity that can be pledged in each area. Currently, it is the same as the maximum FHA loan in the area. It is important to realize, however, that a borrower can access only a portion of the amount pledged, because future interest will increase the loan balance.

Consider the example of a couple, both spouses age 75. If their house is appraised at $100,000—and if that is within the area's maximum—they can receive a $41,600 line of credit. It can be used immediately or figured as a term or lifetime annuity.

Participants also pay closing costs, including an insurance premium that is paid in two parts. First, 2 percent of the home's pledged value is due at closing. Second, an annual fee of 0.5 percent is charged on the loan balance.

Currently, the FHA allows lenders to set interest rates on the state level. As more lenders participate, competition should keep rates in line.

Wisely, the FHA pilot program requires would-be borrowers to meet with counselors to discuss whether they should participate in the program and which option would suit them best. This eases concerns of critics who worry that borrowers who choose the tenure option could be left with little equity and little income.

Participants also need to realize that reverse mortgages can rapidly eat up home equity it took decades to build.

"I advise senior citizens to be certain that they have other assets available if they are planning to go the reverse mortgage route," warned Deborah Ann Ford, professor of economics and finance at the University of Baltimore. "Otherwise, if they are forced to sell their homes eventually, they may not have the resources to live comfortably."

Private Programs

Another type of reverse mortgage was developed by Prudential-Bache Securities in New Jersey in 1984.

Under the program, an annuity payment is made

monthly for the participant's lifetime, and the homeowner agrees to pay the lender a percentage of the increase in the house's value over the term of the annuity. If the home appreciates substantially, the lender benefits. Otherwise the borrower does better.

The amount of the annuity is based on the homeowner's age, the home's market value, and the owner's equity in the property. The entire property need not be committed to the plan.

Though programs such as this have carved out niches in the market, they are unlikely to rival the FHA plan in sheer volume if they take off—as their designers hope they will.

CHAPTER 17
CREATIVE FINANCING

Creative financing is a high-flying route to home ownership. It isn't weighted down by the baggage of a traditional mortgage. Nor is it tethered by the protection of an old-fashioned home loan.

One way to buy a home without a mortgage is to purchase on contract and let the seller provide short-term balloon loan financing at a below-market rate. Balloon loans also are available from traditional mortgage makers, such as mortgage bankers and savings and loan associations. Another way is to assume, or take over, the payments on the seller's mortgage.

When home-loan rates are as high as the ionosphere and mortgage money is as tight as a seat in coach class, financing devices such as contract sales, mortgage assumptions, seller-held balloon loans, and second mortgages soar.

As simple as creative financing sounds, legal experts say that it often may have more inherent risks than tiptoeing on a tightrope without a safety net.

BURSTING BALLOONS

Take a balloon loan, for example. It is attractive because it offers a below-market rate and no closing points—if made by a seller. A lender will charge points at closing, but the rate will be below those on 15-year and 30-year loans. A typical balloon requires a lump-sum payment at the end of a specified term, usually three, five, or seven years. The balloon is said to "pop" at the end of the period.

Consumer advocates warn that home buyers who take off on a home-sale deal funded with a balloon may be floating over tough terrain. If the balloon bursts at an inconvenient time, the buyer could fall into a deep financial chasm.

"What happens when interest rates are higher, not lower, when the balloon comes due?" asks Marshall J. Moltz, a Chicago real estate lawyer. "And what happens if the buyer's income doesn't increase enough for him to qualify for a conventional loan from a bank or savings and loan?"

If rates are high when the balloon bursts, a buyer's alternatives include getting a conventional mortgage at sky-high rates or renegotiating the balloon at a higher rate. If the balloon is extended by a conventional lender, additional closing points often are charged. If the lender—the seller or conventional lender—won't extend the loan, the homeowner could face foreclosure and could lose the house. And if rates are high, there won't be a squadron of buyers waiting to descend upon your house. If you have to sell, you could end up taking a big loss.

Another depressing thought is that balloons were the predominant form of real estate financing that blew thousands of Americans out of their houses during the 1930s.

In times of high mortgage rates, Moltz said, the only protection for a borrower is writing an automatic extension of the balloon in the contract. For example, specify that the loan be extended three years at an interest rate 0.5 percentage point higher than during the original length of the mortgage.

"The seller also has to protect himself in a contract deal," said Moltz. "His lawyer should put a rider into the contract saying that if mortgage rates drop, the buyer has to go out and get a mortgage." That way the seller can take his or her money and be free of the house.

With enough variations of creative financing to fill the basket of a large hot-air balloon, a guide is necessary to help buyers and sellers avoid tripping over a bad deal and tumbling into financial oblivion. Here is a rundown on a few of them:

MORTGAGE ASSUMPTION

Before you buy real estate, ask a seller if his or her mortgage is assumable. It's possible to save thousands of dollars if you can take over a seller's low-rate mortgage and smaller payments.

But don't be lured near a financial canyon without knowing of possible problems that could put you over the edge. For example, a sale based on an assumption could be illegal if the mortgage contains a clause requiring full repayment of the loan if the home is sold. Courts have ruled that, to be effective, a due-on-sale clause must be written into both the mortgage document and the note.

Most due-on-sale mortgages require the loan to be paid off in full if the property is sold on contract, Moltz said. The seller could be slapped with an interest penalty if the lender learns of an illegal contract deal.

And the low-rate loan that attracted you to the home will vanish like a mirage, leaving you with payments you can't afford.

One way to avoid due-on-sale provisions is to assume a home loan backed by Uncle Sam. All FHA-insured and VA-guaranteed mortgages are assumable. Also, most conventional mortgages that were taken out 10 or more years ago can be assumed.

The problem with the conventional loans that old is that the value of most homes has doubled or tripled since the old mortgage was taken out. Thus, the balance on the mortgage is not nearly enough for the new buyer.

That's why so many lending institutions permitted "blended" mortgages during the early 1980s. In return for the seller paying off the low-rate loan, the lender initiated a loan for the buyer at an interest rate above that of the old mortgage but lower than the prevailing market rate.

BALLOON LOANS

The interest rate on balloons made by conventional lenders is usually fixed and always lower than a long-term, fixed-rate mortgage, because the loan is paid off faster. Payments are set up as if you would pay off the loan over 30 years. However, the entire principal amount is due at the end of the specified shorter period.

Maximum loan amounts can vary from $187,600 to $300,000, and down payments run anywhere from 5 percent to 25 percent. Lenders usually charge a $250 closing fee plus closing costs of 2.5 percent to 3 percent of the loan amount. With a down payment of less than 20 percent, private mortgage insurance is required.

CONTRACT SALES

Most contract sales involve a negotiated down payment and a short-term balloon loan provided by the seller. The loan is like the balloon made by conventional lenders, but it may carry a lower interest rate, and no points are charged at closing.

Under the agreement, the seller holds title to the property until the terms of the contract are met. The contract will spell out the amount of down payment, length of contract, and the principal and interest payment to be made by the purchaser.

Although the monthly payments in a contract deal are based on a 25- or 30-year amortization schedule, most contract deals call for a lump-sum balloon payment at a specified time.

Contract buyers do not have the same legal rights as other mortgage borrowers. The biggest risk for a contract buyer is a fast foreclosure triggered by late monthly payments. While it may take as long as a year to foreclose on a mortgage in some states, a contract buyer can be foreclosed on in as little as 60 to 90 days.

If the contract deal is tied to an existing mortgage, problems can arise for the buyer if the seller doesn't meet loan obligations. Experts advise that the buyer's lawyer make provisions in the contract that allow the buyer to pay the lender directly if the seller fails to pay his or her mortgage.

Experts also recommend strongly that the deed be placed in escrow at a title insurance company. This avoids an estate problem if the seller dies before the contract is paid off. Obviously, a real estate lawyer is invaluable for the buyer—and the seller—in a contract sale.

Beware if the property is held in a land trust. In

Illinois and other states, if you miss a payment on the contract deal, your beneficial interest in the trust could be sold in as little as 15 days. It's just like missing a payment on an automobile.

PURCHASE-MONEY MORTGAGES

If the owner holds title to the property without a lien and does not need the cash from the sale all at once, he or she can write a mortgage contract and charge the borrower interest. The rate is often far below prevailing interest rates on this seller-held first mortgage because the seller wants to sell the home in a weak housing market.

The biggest difference between this and a contract sale with a balloon is that under a purchase-money mortgage, the buyer gets deed and title to the home at closing.

For unsophisticated sellers, the biggest pitfalls lie in setting the rate too low and in collection risks, Moltz said. "The purchase-money mortgage contract must call for late-payment charges or interest penalties to keep the buyer honest," he recommended.

SELLER-HELD SECOND MORTGAGES

A second mortgage is a loan secured by property that already is secured by a loan—the first mortgage or deed of trust. If the buyer can't obtain a large enough mortgage to purchase a home—or wants to borrow as little as possible at market rates—the seller may extend a second mortgage to make up the difference.

Often this lasts for 1 to 5 years, although the payments on the second mortgage are kept low by figuring them as if the loan would last 25 or 30 years. The balance is due in a balloon payment, or lump sum, at the end of the loan period.

Many lenders, however, won't allow a second mortgage if they learn about it, because they fear this would reduce the borrower's ability to repay the first loan. In an effort to conceal the second mortgage from the primary lender, Moltz said, most seconds are recorded after closing.

Also, the seller holding the second mortgage can be shortchanged if the buyer doesn't make payments on the first mortgage. In case of foreclosure, the holder of the second mortgage would be paid only after the primary lender gets all its money.

BUYDOWNS

A creative financing technique often overlooked by purchasers is provided through mortgage buydowns, or subsidies, from private sellers or builders trying to sell a house quickly. The seller pays a lump sum up front to the lender, who figures this in while setting the monthly payments for the first two or three years.

Buydowns make the first two or three years of home ownership financially easier. But remember, there is no free lunch. Usually the cost of the buydown is added to the price of the house. And while mortgages are for 15 or 30 years, buydowns usually run for only 3 years. At the end of the period, the buyer must either obtain new financing and pay off the loan or pay the rate stated in the agreement.

Buydowns may be worth the extra cost if you plan to stay in the home for at least as long as the buydown is in effect. If not, you are paying the full cost of the buydown but not using it.

PREPAYING A MORTGAGE

One of the most creative ways to rapidly pay off a home or at least to build equity quickly is by taking out a 30-year conventional or government-backed mortgage, then prepaying the loan. Every dollar of the prepayment would go to reduce the principal of the loan.

It seldom occurs to homeowners to pay off their mortgage ahead of schedule, because they can't imagine that an extra $50 a month makes much of a difference. But even a small increase in payments that goes exclusively to reduce principal can put thousands of dollars in your pocket over the long term and reduce the length of the mortgage by years.

Tell the bank what you're doing (and be sure that prepayments won't generate a penalty), then include an extra amount in each mortgage check marked "for reduction of principal."

The beauty of prepayment is that you don't have to lock yourself into the larger payments that a shorter-term amortization schedule would require. If you're not sure that you can handle the burden of large monthly payments on a 15-year loan, take the 30-year loan and try to make regular or lump sum prepayments whenever possible. But you are free to choose when an extra payment fits into your budget.

One prepayment rule of thumb is to add to your monthly principal and interest payment an amount equal to the next month's principal payment. You will be given a table outlining each of your 360 monthly payments—and how they are split between principal and interest—when you get a 30-year mortgage.

By making the next month's principal payment in advance, you will be reducing the balance upon which interest is calculated monthly. That means that each future monthly payment—though fixed in amount—will put more toward principal than it would have.

If you follow this procedure regularly, you can save tens of thousands of dollars and cut years off your mortgage.

Though exact calculations of how much this will speed up your loan are complicated, your lender should send you an annual statement detailing how much principal remains. Compare this to the table you received at closing. If at the end of year two your principal balance is equal to year four on your table, you already have cut two years off your mortgage. Your savings in interest would be 24 times your monthly payment.

Before you start, make sure your promissory note does not specifically prohibit prepayment of principal. Some lenders restrict the number of principal prepayments allowed each year. If it is not a violation of the note, you do not need the approval or consent of your lender before you prepay.

It also is important to enclose a note with your mortgage payment informing the lender about the amount of the principal prepayment. For your records, itemize the exact distribution covered in the payment, preferably on the check.

ZERO PERCENT FINANCING

Zero percent financing really may be as good as it sounds. This financing method is rarely seen except when sellers are anxious to make a sale during periods of high interest rates. No financing fees are charged during the one- to five-year term of a zero percent loan. You simply repay the principal rapidly.

One Chicago-area builder, Sundance Homes, used this method to sell suburban homes in 1982, when fixed rates hovered around 15 percent. Buyers were required to make a down payment of at least 33 percent of the purchase price and had five years of fixed monthly payments to pay off the rest of the loan. "Today, these buyers own their homes outright, while many of their neighbors still are making hefty principal and interest payments," said Maurice Sanderman, president of Sundance Homes.

Individual sellers also used this method during the early 1980s, but used much shorter terms.

If zero percent financing sounds too good to be true, consider Uncle Sam's position. The federal government allowed buyers who used zero percent financing to consider 10 percent of the principal payment as tax-deductible interest. No one really charges zero percent interest, Uncle Sam says.

That's the first question a borrower should ask: Has the cost of financing been added to the price of the home? In times of unexpectedly weak buyer demand, the financing cost may come from a seller's profit, though perhaps the seller would have cut the price if you had more usual financing.

The second consideration involves cash flow. Because an extraordinarily large down payment is required and the majority of the monthly payment goes to principal, not tax-deductible interest (unlike most mortgage plans), a borrower must have substantial monthly income to handle the payments. After five years, however, the borrower owns the property free and clear.

CHAPTER 18

PARENTS HELP OUT

For as long as there have been parents and children, there have been parents helping grown children get their own home. In previous centuries, that may have meant helping fell trees or drive nails. Today it may mean providing assistance with the down payment, co-signing the mortgage, or even buying the home together.

"My parents knew we were looking for a house," said a 27-year-old Chicago-area woman. "And they knew we couldn't afford to get what we wanted in this house."

So the parents, who had helped their son and daughter-in-law buy a home several years before, increased the down payment for their daughter, son-in-law, and grandson, who bought a suburban duplex.

Like these parents, millions of parents nationwide are making the American dream of home ownership come true despite rising home prices.

"In the period I bought my home, in 1971, most

young Americans needed help from their parents," said Bob Brunner, executive vice president of Talman Home Mortgage Corp. in Chicago. "I don't think that's changed."

The runup in housing prices in recent years has increased the equity for many longtime homeowners, making it possible for them to help their children.

"When you're doing OK and taking care of your own personal needs, you can take care of your children," said Sam Pincich, director of real estate lending for the U.S. League of Savings Institutions, a trade group. "There are a lot of people whose parents—or two sets of parents—have helped them buy these homes."

The addition of many women to the work force when their children are in high school or college also adds to a family's disposable income once the college years are over, he said.

"They have the capacity to do that and are doing that more than in the past," said Pincich, who is in his fifties. "In my parents' generation, they didn't have the capacity to help because they were barely getting by themselves."

Because lenders often don't know of the help parents are providing, it's impossible to tell what percentage of first-time buyers have parental help, but it's clearly widespread.

Here are some of the ways it's done.

DOWN PAYMENT HELP

"Very often, a couple can afford the mortgage payments but haven't been able to accumulate the down payment," said the U.S. League's Pincich. "They need help with the down payment."

This can be an outright gift or a loan.

A gift means the parent has neither an obligation to see that the loan is repaid nor any claim to the money. On a gift, the lender will require an affidavit stating that the money is a gift. On mortgages that are, or might be, sold to investors by the lender, Pincich said, the following conditions have become an industry standard:

- The agreement must be in writing, indicating what relative gave the funds, how much was given, what property is being bought, and that repayment is not required or expected.

- The affidavit must be signed by both the donor and the recipient.

- There must be written evidence of the transfer of funds, such as a canceled check and a deposit slip.

- On a purchase with less than 20 percent down, at least 5 percent must be from the borrower.

The gift, if it makes the down payment at least 20 percent, will help the buyer avoid paying private mortgage insurance, which could add half a percentage point to the interest rate.

On a family loan, the repayment terms and the lender determine how it will be treated. If the loan is to be repaid in a lump sum in 10 or 20 years or upon the sale of the home, Bell Federal Savings in Chicago doesn't consider it in qualifying the applicant. The S&L does not sell its loans to investors, and thus has more leeway, said Robert G. Rowan, senior vice president of the mortgage loan division. If monthly repayment is required, Bell will figure it as a monthly bill and use it to determine whether a buyer qualifies.

Talman Home, however, figures what it would take

to pay off the loan in monthly payments over the next ten years, and includes those figures in making sure long-term debt payments don't exceed 33 percent of monthly income.

A loan not only helps the child get the home before prices increase but also establishes some responsibility.

"Sometimes, it's hard to give people things without taking something away from them," Pinich said. "The person that receives the gift may feel diminished. From a relationship standpoint, maybe the children will feel better with an obligation, even if it's 20 years down the road."

RATE BUYDOWN

Whether a loan or a gift, a rate buydown has a dramatic impact on payments for the first few years, which often are the most difficult for new homeowners as they adjust to the costs and responsibilities of a home. The parents pay a sum of money up front, and the rate on which payments are based is reduced for a specified, temporary period.

For example, a 3-2-1 buydown is one choice. In the first year, the effective rate is 3 percentage points below the stated rate on the loan; in the second year, 2 percentage points; in the third year, 1 percentage point.

With prevailing rates on a 30-year, fixed-rate loan at 11.125 percent, the first-year rate would be 8.125 percent; the second, 9.125 percent; and the third, 10.125 percent. In years 4 through 30, the rate would be 11.125 percent.

On a $100,000 mortgage, the payments for principal and interest would be $742 in year one, $814 in year two, then $887, and eventually $961. Of course, this costs money up front. On the $100,000 loan, it would cost about $5,300.

While a larger down payment will reduce the mortgage amount and thus the monthly payments, a buydown will drop the payment even more—but only for a few years. Also, the lender may qualify a borrower based on the first-year payment rate, meaning less income is needed to get the loan.

There's a catch to buydowns: if the house is sold before the buydown years are over, you'll have paid the full buydown fee without getting the full benefits.

PAYING MORE POINTS AT CLOSING

Lenders generally have a sliding scale so that the more points you pay at closing, the lower the rate over the life of a fixed-rate loan. One point is equal to 1 percent of the loan amount.

As with a buydown, the rate on the loan is lower. Unlike a buydown, it's not all that much lower but will last for the life of the loan.

For example, one lender was charging 0.75 points on an 11.375 percent, 30-year fixed loan, 1.75 points on an 11.125 percent loan, and 2.75 points on a 10.875 percent loan.

Unfortunately, most buyers, especially first-timers, don't stay in a home through the end of a mortgage, so they don't get the full benefit of the lower rate. Also, the money spent on points could be used as a down payment, helping buyers reach the magical 5 percent or 10 percent down that some lenders require.

CO-SIGNING THE LOAN

If the parents co-sign the loan, this may not require any money up front—or ever. The children receive the coupon book for the mortgage, but the parents sign that they'll pay the loan in case the children fall behind. This makes the loan more attractive to a lender.

In co-signing situations, lenders will scrutinize the financial situation of both the children and the parents.

Co-signing is especially attractive for parents who don't want to or can't plunk down a chunk of cash up front but have available income. Co-signing a loan has a much greater risk for parents than giving or lending money, because they are on the hook for the whole mortgage and may have to sell the house.

To protect themselves, parents should have their names on the title. That way, they can sell the home if they have to take over payments.

HOLDING THE MORTGAGE

For the parents to hold the mortgage, a family must be wealthy or have good timing. For example, if the parents or grandparents just sold their last home and are looking for a reasonable, steady return, this might work. Or it's a way to use a big inheritance.

The advantages are immediate. In loans between private parties, there are no points. That saves $3,000 on a $100,000 loan.

In addition, the rate can be lower, because parents can get the same return as on a certificate of deposit while charging the children rates lower than a lender's because they don't have all the overhead costs.

The Internal Revenue Service, however, assumes that the loan is at market rates. Each month, it sets a *minimum* rate for loans originated in that month. In March 1989, the rate compounded annually for loans of nine years or longer was 9.14 percent. For up to five years, it was 9.3 percent, and for five up to nine years, it was 9.31 percent.

So, if in March 1989 parents made a $100,000, 30-year mortgage loan to their children, the IRS would charge the parents tax on the income based on 9.14 percent. For such instances, the IRS has a separate line on Schedule A of the 1040 return to list mortgage interest to someone other than a lending institution.

To make sure such a mortgage is set up properly, contact a lawyer and maybe an accountant.

EQUITY SHARING

The use of equity sharing usually involves cash up front, co-signing a mortgage, rental income, and depreciation.

The parents own part of the home and rent it to the children. The parents may make part of the mortgage payment and declare the rent as income, but they can deduct their share of property taxes and can depreciate their share of the property.

Meanwhile, the children own part of the house and can deduct on federal income tax forms their share of the mortgage interest and property taxes. They also must pay the parents a fair market rent for their share of the house.

On a hypothetical $100,000 home, 50-50 equity sharing could work like this, although many variations are possible:

The parents would put down $10,000, and the parents and children each would make $500 of the monthly payment for mortgage principal, interest, taxes, and insurance. In addition, the children would make a monthly payment of $300 to rent their parents' half of the house.

At the end of the year, the parents declare rental income of $3,600 but deduct depreciation and property taxes on their half. The children deduct half of the interest and property taxes.

At a specified time, or perhaps when the house is sold, the children would be required to repay the $10,000 down payment and to pay the parents 50 percent of the home's appreciation.

Most parents and children would be put off by the complexity of equity sharing, but it can provide assistance for the children and tax breaks for the parents. It also can get cash-short children into a home and help make the payments easier to take.

This choice definitely requires the expertise of a real estate attorney.

EMOTIONAL CONSIDERATIONS

In addition to the dollars and cents, any parental help involves emotional considerations. Will the child or the child and spouse be better off—in financial and maturity terms—with or without the help?

"First of all, try to be a little unemotional about it," said the U.S. League's Pincich. "Think through a number of possibilities. What happens if the marriage dissolves? What happens when they sell that house and want to move up?"

Here are some suggestions that may make parents feel comfortable with giving or lending money:

- If the children don't object, go along to look at homes, either new or resale. Especially if you haven't bought recently, the experience will give you an understanding of housing prices.

- Before committing to a child who hasn't shown much responsibility, have the child set up an account that will be for the down payment. You can offer to match $3 or $4 for every $1 put in by the child.

- Set up a repayment schedule. On a $10,000 loan, for example, a monthly payment of $140 would retire the loan in six years, if you didn't charge any interest.

- Put in writing how much you have given and what the terms are—even if the lender knows nothing about it.

Putting the terms in writing has two benefits. First, each family will get credit if divorce splits the "ours" into "yours" and "mine." Ghoulish as it sounds, this happens to half of all marriages. Second, parents and children both know exactly what the deal is up front. This reduces the chance of misunderstandings—and bad feelings—later on.

Once all the financial terms have been ironed out, parents can provide two other kinds of assistance to new homeowners: moral and physical. And these are priceless.

CHAPTER 19
COMPUTERIZED MORTGAGE HUNTING: THE WAVE OF THE FUTURE

Computerized home-loan hunting will become commonplace in the 1990s, mortgage experts say. Indeed, such systems already have linked thousands of buyers with lenders through real estate companies nationwide.

Even before a buyer decides on the house he or she wants, it is possible to prequalify for a mortgage at a participating real estate broker's office using a computerized system.

The borrower provides personal financial information typically required by mortgage lenders. This would include the amount of the down payment to be made, income, debts, and the monthly payment the borrower can afford.

The numbers are fed into a computer, which produces a range of prices that the buyer can afford. The computer system lists up-to-the-minute mortgage information on interest rates, related points, requirements to qualify, and other information on available loans.

The buyer then views mortgages that are sorted by loan type, interest rate, annual percentage rate, and down payment requirements. From this menu, the borrower chooses a loan.

For example, if you earn $40,000 a year and have monthly auto loan and credit card debt payments totaling $262, the printout would show that you can qualify for a monthly mortgage principal and interest payment of $833. (As discussed in Chapter 4, you could also figure that 25 percent of your gross monthly income is available for principal and interest payments. In this case, 25 percent of $3,333 per month is $833.) Based on this monthly payment, you should be able to qualify for a 30-year, fixed-rate mortgage of $91,100 at an interest rate of 10.5 percent.

However, if lenders are offering mortgages at interest rates of 10 percent, you could qualify for a $94,900 loan. If you choose a 15-year fixed loan at 10 percent, you would qualify for a loan of only $77,500.

Once the buyer selects a home, he or she reviews all the financing options available, then chooses a mortgage and fills out a loan application. Verification forms are entered into the computer and electronically transmitted to the lender. The original signed documents are messengered to the lender from the real estate office.

The computer system allows the lender to begin processing the mortgage application immediately, thus reducing the time it takes to close the loan.

For home buyers, the computerized system makes a sometimes frustrating task much easier and may provide a lower-cost loan than might otherwise be found. For participating lenders, the system provides customers who might otherwise have gone to another lender. For real estate brokers, the system facilitates the process of selling homes, gives salespeople an edge over competitors in attracting clients, and may provide additional income.

Differences among services provided by computerized loan hunters lie in who pays for the service, who provides the mortgage products, and who operates the system.

Perhaps the highest-profile computerized system, MortgagePower lists only loan products of Citicorp Loan Corporation. About 4,000 users, generally real estate brokers, pay a monthly fee to gain access. Borrowers can receive application approval in 15 minutes. Brokers are able to pass the cost on to home buyers in the form of a fee for finding the right mortgage and processing an application, but not all brokers charge a fee.

With franchise operations such as Century 21, Prudential, and *ERA* and large chains such as Coldwell Banker Real Estate dominating the resale real estate market in many cities, computerized mortgage services are certain to become more widely available. In fact, the computer software needed for mortgage hunts and other operations is one of the attractions that independent brokers see in franchises.

CHAPTER 20

TWENTY COMMON QUESTIONS AND ANSWERS ABOUT HOME LOANS

1. How can I figure how much mortgage I can afford?

When lenders figure how much of a loan a home buyer can afford, they use general rules of thumb. They say your mortgage principal and interest payments should not exceed 25 percent of your gross monthly income. When real estate taxes and homeowners' insurance are added, your monthly payments should not exceed 28 percent of your gross income.

Total housing costs plus other long-term debts, such as car payments, student loans, and credit card obligations, should not exceed 33 percent of gross monthly income.

If you can qualify within these guidelines, you should be able to afford a home.

2. Should I take out a mortgage now or wait for rates to go lower?

If you know for certain where rates are going, you

should be a millionaire in the bond markets of Wall Street. In January 1989 economists were predicting 30-year, fixed-rate mortgages would be going for 11.5 percent to 12 percent by the middle of the year. By June, however, the average loan was at 10 percent.

In other words, ordinary consumers should grab a rate that makes sense. There's no telling when rates will go up or down. If the financing works out to be a good, affordable deal, take it and be happy. Maybe you won't get the lowest rate of the year, but by waiting for the "perfect" time, you may miss the boat if rates go higher. Also, that home you like today may be sold to someone else tomorrow—probably at a higher price.

3. Where should I start to look for a mortgage?
Local S&Ls are a good place to start your search for a home loan, because they specialize in long-term mortgages. Also, they tend to be more sensitive to borrowers' needs because they want to service the loan and maintain a good customer relationship. They want to sell their mortgage borrowers their other services, such as savings accounts, home-improvement loans, and certificates of deposit.

However, you may pay a slightly higher rate at an S&L, because most of them handle a lower volume of business than mortgage companies accommodate. And mortgage companies handle only one business: mortgages.

During a strong mortgage market, an S&L may process and approve a loan faster than a mortgage company because the S&L may know the local system better.

4. Because lenders seem to be so competitive, aren't all their rates about the same?
No. Like supermarkets and department stores, lend-

ing institutions have different costs and desired profit margins. Also, they try to establish different client bases. Consequently, lenders' offerings can differ in rates, points, and fees.

5. How many lenders should I call for loan-rate quotes when shopping for a mortgage?

An old rule of thumb was three. That was true in the days of homogeneous lenders and mortgages. In the deregulated and highly competitive market that exists now, three probably is too few.

Why not get out your local phone book and phone every lender in there? Sure, this will take a little bit of time. But consider that every $10 in monthly payments means 180 or 360 months at $10. That's $1,800 to $3,600 over the course of a 15-year loan and a 30-year loan, respectively. So, calling lots of lenders may be a very good investment.

6. How much will it cost to take out a mortgage?

That depends on the lender, but figure on paying about 4.5 percent of the home's costs in points and fees. When you compare loans from different lenders, look at all costs, not just rates and points.

When you talk to a potential lender, ask which of the following fees apply to loans: points, title search, title exam insurance, application fee, credit report, appraisal fee, loan origination fee, recording taxes, and private mortgage insurance. Also, you probably should hire a real estate lawyer.

When you close, you also will have to prepay the first year's homeowners' insurance premium and pro-rated property taxes. Ask your realty agent if the seller will pay any of these fees. Also ask if there are any other fees the lender charges.

7. *Is it a good idea to lock in the interest rate that is in effect when I make my loan application? Is there a fee for this?*

Ask exactly when the rate you are applying for will be established. With rates fluctuating daily, a homeowner should determine whether the rate will be the one available on the day of the application or the one available on the day of the closing. If a lender will give you the rate quoted at application time for no additional fee, you probably would be wise to take it.

Some lenders, however, charge up to a full point extra at application time if a homeowner wants to be locked in to a chosen rate if closing is within a specified period of time. If rates move lower, this money would be wasted. Sometimes, locking in the rate doesn't pay even if rates move higher. In 1986, thousands of borrowers who paid for a locked rate still got burned because of mortgage processing delays. Sixty-day rate commitments expired, and borrowers had to pay current market rates, which happened to be higher than at application time.

Other times, however, locking in pays off handsomely. One home buyer in the western suburbs of Chicago applied for a 30-year, fixed-rate loan in May. The lender guaranteed the rate for 60 days with no fee. Because the buyer had to take time to sell his town house, he paid 0.5 percent of the loan amount in points to lock in the 10-percent rate for an extra 30 days. By the time he closed in August, rates had climbed to 10.5 percent. Locking in paid off.

8. *Should I choose a fixed-rate loan or an adjustable-rate mortgage?*

That question cannot be answered simply. If you intend to stay in your home for just a few years, chances are the adjustable-rate mortgage will cost you less. The first-year rate probably will be at least 2 percentage points lower than for a fixed-rate loan, because lenders want to attract ARM business. In the second year, the ARM rate probably will increase to about the level of the fixed-rate loan. The lower rate in the first year makes the ARM a short-term bargain.

However, if you intend to stay in the home for at least several years, there are different considerations. If you don't mind the risk of fluctuating rates and your budget can absorb payment increases, you may want to stick with the ARM and see where rates go. Or you may prefer the peace of mind of a fixed-rate loan; over the long haul, the ARM could go several points higher—or lower—than the fixed.

Without a crystal ball, it's impossible to tell where rates will be a few years from now. With a fixed-rate loan, you know what you'll be paying each and every month for a very long time. With an ARM, you know only the maximum and perhaps the minimum rates you'll be paying—and the maximum is much higher than the current fixed rates.

9. What's better—a 15-year mortgage or a 30-year loan?

More and more home buyers consider 15-year loans when lower rates bring the payments within financial reach. The interest savings are dramatic with a 15-year loan. And it's amazing how much faster equity is built up in a 15-year loan. That equity is helpful if you are planning to move up to a larger home or just want to be done making mortgage payments. Also, lenders usually charge a slightly lower rate on a 15-year loan than on a 30-year mortgage.

This example may make the difference clearer: On a $100,000 loan at 9.75 percent for 15 years, you would owe $81,000 after five years. Had you chosen a 30-year loan at 10 percent, you would owe $96,600 after five years.

The difference is even more dramatic after 15 years. You'd have paid off that 15-year loan, but you'd still owe $81,700 on the 30-year mortgage.

However, if you can't afford the higher payments of a 15-year mortgage, a 30-year loan will give you the advantage of higher federal income tax deductions for mortgage interest.

10. I just finished law school and landed a well-paying job. But I have very little money to put down on a home. Also, I have lots of school loans to pay off in the next few years. Am I out of luck on a home until then?

Not necessarily. Graduated-payment mortgages were designed for people just like you. The payments start out relatively low, but increase annually for a specified period. This allows you to have a home and get on your feet financially. There are substantial tax benefits in the early years of the loan that will help you every April 15.

As your payments increase, you start to really build up equity. This equity will be helpful in buying a bigger home down the road. One word of caution: If you can, avoid graduated-payment mortgages that feature negative amortization, or you can end up owing more than you did at the beginning of the loan.

11. Will my mortgage payment be more expensive if I can't come up with a 20 percent down payment?

If your down payment is less than 20 percent, you will be required to pay a private mortgage insurance premium. PMI should not be confused with life insurance; PMI paid by the borrower merely protects the lender.

With a 10 percent down payment, you would have to

pay 0.4 percent of the mortgage amount at closing to cover the first year's premium. On a $90,000 mortgage, that's $360.

The second year's PMI with a 10 percent down payment will be 0.34 percent of the loan balance. On the $90,000 loan, it would be about $300—paid in 12 monthly installments of about $25. PMI also can be paid up front. On a 10 percent down payment, the one-time premium would be 2.95 percent of the loan amount.

PMI payments usually continue until you have paid off enough of the mortgage to reach 20 percent of the purchase price.

12. Why do I have to pay points and fees when taking out a mortgage?

Lenders say borrowers have to pay the freight of originating the loan. Mortgage fees, like the price of a new car, are negotiable. They tend to be substantially higher than the actual cost of doing the work because lenders charge what the market will bear. When rates are low and borrowing activity is high, some lenders cash in. So, shop around.

13. Am I better off paying more points at closing to get a lower rate on the loan?

First, you should realize that the long-run difference between the choices is not all that substantial. Otherwise, the lender would not be so willing to offer more than one choice.

By paying more points, however, you are tying up more of your money up front. If you move within two or three years, those up-front costs are gone. But if you prefer to have a smaller monthly obligation and expect to stay for more than five years, go ahead and pay the points.

14. How long will it take to close on a mortgage from the time I make the application?

It's impossible to say how long this will take, but be prepared for a wait. Once you begin the process, however, you usually can lock in a rate with the lender.

There are a number of things you can do to speed up the process. These include paying the loan application fee immediately, alerting your employer that an employment verification is on the way, getting copies of your tax forms for the last two years, providing the lender with account number and address for bank and stock accounts and credit cards. Also, you should provide the lender with names and addresses on all loans you have paid off.

If you need a loan quickly, lenders often can accommodate you.

15. Do I need an attorney to handle the closing of my home?

You are entering a contract that will obligate you to repay perhaps hundreds of thousands of dollars. You should have an attorney involved in such a substantial undertaking.

16. Do I need to hire a home inspector to check over the property before I buy it?

It is an excellent idea for the buyer of a home to hire an independent engineer or home inspector to check the property for termites and potential structural and mechanical defects. The inspector also will note small matters such as low water pressure and cracked window panes. This usually costs $250. Attach a rider to the sales contract making purchase contingent upon the inspector's approval.

17. We are a retired couple with grown children. We don't want to sell our home, which is paid off. How can we tap our home's equity to meet expenses?

One possibility is a Grannie Mae mortgage. It involves selling your home to your children, then renting it back from them at fair market value under a lifetime lease. The proceeds are invested, and you receive a monthly income check for the rest of your lives. The rent payment is given to your children, who pay the mortgage. In addition, the Federal Housing Administration has launched a pilot program for reverse equity mortgages. It may be awhile before such loans are widely available.

18. My husband and I have saved only a few thousand dollars. How can we buy a home?

If you have a steady job and earn enough to qualify for a Federal Housing Administration–insured mortgage, you can buy an $80,000 home with a down payment of as little as $3,500. You also will have to pay a loan origination fee of 1 percent of the loan amount, plus another 1 percent for closing costs—a total of $1,530. In addition, there may be discount points, which you may split with the seller.

19. I served in the military in Vietnam and bought a home under the GI Bill afterward. I paid off the loan when I sold that house. Can I buy another home with a VA loan?

Veterans whose previous loans have been paid in full are eligible for new loans guaranteed by the Department of Veterans Affairs. If a veteran sells a home purchased with a VA mortgage and the buyer assumes the mortgage, the veteran can get another VA loan only after the first is paid off.

Because it has been years since you used a VA loan,

you may be surprised that you can borrow up to $144,000 without making any down payment. If you make a $10,000 down payment, you could get a loan of up to $184,000—if your income is enough to handle the payments.

20. We are interested in buying a home but can't qualify for a mortgage. What are the dangers of buying on contract?

Contract buyers do not have the same legal rights as other mortgage borrowers. In particular, late monthly payments can trigger a fast foreclosure. While it may take as long as a year to foreclose on a mortgage, a contract buyer can be foreclosed on in as little as 60 to 90 days.

Another problem is that sellers rarely even consider a contract sale except during weak housing markets. You may have a hard time finding someone who doesn't want all the money immediately.

A final point: A lender isn't disqualifying you for a loan because he or she doesn't like you. Over time, lenders learned that buyers with insufficient income frequently are foreclosed on. Make sure you have enough income to cover your home purchase, or you could end up losing everything you put into a house—and ruin your credit history, too.

APPENDIX

LOAN AMORTIZATION AND LOAN PROGRESS TABLES

HOW TO USE LOAN AMORTIZATION TABLES

Every mortgage borrower should know how to use a loan amortization table. Once you know current interest rates, it's easy to figure out what mortgage payment it will take to pay off a loan over 15 or 30 years.

This is how lenders do it: Look across from the interest rate and down from the mortgage amount. Where they intersect is the monthly payment for principal and interest. For example, the monthly principal and interest for a 30-year loan at 10 percent for $60,000 would be $526.55.

If your mortgage amount is not one of those listed, this procedure is just a little bit harder. Look across from the interest rate to the cost for a $1,000 loan. Then multiply that number by the amount of your loan in thousands. For example, a 30-year loan at 10 percent

Loan Amortization And Loan Progress Tables 163

would cost $8.78 per $1,000. For a $66,000 loan, it would cost $8.78 times 66, or $579.48.

Monthly Payments to Amortize 30-Year Fixed-Rate Loan

Interest Rate	\$1,000	\$40,000	\$50,000	\$60,000	\$70,000	\$100,000
8.00%	$ 7.34	$293.51	$366.89	$440.26	$513.64	$ 733.77
8.25	7.52	300.51	375.64	450.76	525.89	751.27
8.50	7.69	307.57	384.46	461.35	538.24	768.92
8.75	7.87	314.69	393.36	472.03	550.70	786.71
9.00	8.05	321.85	402.32	482.78	563.24	804.63
9.25	8.23	329.08	411.34	493.61	575.88	822.68
9.50	8.41	336.35	420.43	504.52	588.60	840.86
9.75	8.60	343.67	429.58	515.50	601.41	854.16
10.00	8.78	351.03	438.79	526.55	614.31	877.58
10.25	8.97	358.45	448.06	537.67	627.28	896.11
10.50	9.15	365.90	457.37	548.85	640.32	914.74
10.75	9.34	373.40	466.75	560.09	653.44	933.49
11.00	9.53	380.93	476.17	571.40	666.63	952.33
11.25	9.72	388.51	485.64	582.76	679.89	971.27
11.50	9.91	396.12	495.15	594.18	693.21	990.30
11.75	10.10	403.77	504.71	605.65	706.59	1,009.41
12.00	10.29	411.45	514.31	617.17	720.03	1,028.62
12.50	10.68	426.91	533.63	640.36	747.09	1,067.26
13.00	11.07	442.48	553.10	663.72	774.34	1,106.20
13.50	11.46	458.17	572.71	687.25	801.79	1,145.42
14.00	11.85	473.95	592.44	710.93	829.42	1,184.88
14.50	12.25	489.83	612.28	734.74	857.19	1,224.56
15.00	12.65	505.78	632.23	758.67	885.12	1,264.45

Monthly Payments to Amortize 15-Year Fixed-Rate Loan

Interest Rate	\$1,000	\$40,000	\$50,000	\$60,000	\$70,000	\$100,000
8.00%	$ 9.56	$382.27	$477.83	$573.40	$668.96	$ 955.66
8.25	9.71	388.06	485.08	582.09	679.10	970.15
8.50	9.85	393.90	492.37	590.85	689.32	984.74
8.75	10.00	399.78	499.73	599.67	699.62	999.45
9.00	10.15	405.71	507.14	608.56	709.99	1,014.27
9.25	10.30	411.68	514.60	617.52	720.44	1,029.20
9.50	10.45	417.69	522.12	626.54	730.96	1,044.23
9.75	10.60	423.75	529.69	635.62	741.56	1,059.37

Interest Rate	$1,000	$40,000	$50,000	$60,000	$70,000	$100,000
10.00%	$10.75	$429.85	$537.31	$644.77	$752.23	$1,074.61
10.25	10.90	435.99	544.98	653.98	762.97	1,089.96
10.50	11.06	442.16	552.70	663.24	773.78	1,105.40
10.75	11.21	448.38	560.48	672.57	784.67	1,120.95
11.00	11.37	454.64	568.30	681.96	795.62	1,136.60
11.25	11.53	460.94	576.18	691.41	806.65	1,152.35
11.50	11.69	467.28	584.10	700.92	817.74	1,168.19
11.75	11.85	473.66	592.07	710.48	828.90	1,184.14
12.00	12.01	480.07	600.09	720.11	840.12	1,200.17
12.50	12.33	493.01	616.27	739.52	862.77	1,232.53
13.00	12.66	506.10	632.63	759.15	885.67	1,265.25
13.50	12.99	519.33	649.16	779.00	908.83	1,298.32
14.00	13.32	532.70	665.88	799.05	932.22	1,331.75
14.50	13.66	546.21	682.76	819.31	955.86	1,365.51
15.00	14.00	559.84	699.80	839.76	979.72	1,399.59

HOW TO USE LOAN PROGRESS TABLES

Loan progress tables will help you know how much of your loan will be paid off after set amounts of time have elapsed.

First, find the interest rate of your loan in the left column. Next, in the second column, find the original term—or length—of your loan. Then run your finger across to the year of the loan that you are interested in. The figure represents the amount of principal remaining to be paid off for each $1,000 of your loan. To find the total remaining principal, multiply this number by the amount of your loan in thousands.

For example, after 5 years of a 30-year loan at 10 percent, you would still owe $966 of each $1,000 you borrowed. On a $60,000 loan, you would still owe $966 times 60, or $57,960.

After 20 years on that same 10 percent, 30-year loan, you would still owe $664 of each $1,000 originally borrowed. On that $60,000 loan, you would still owe $664 times 60, or $39,840.

Loan Progress Table

Showing the dollar balance remaining per $1,000 of loan

Interest Rate	Original Term	2	5	8	10	12	15	18	20	22	25
8⅛%	10	859	600	269							
	15	926	789	615	473	307					
	20	957	877	775	692	595	415	186			
	25	973	924	861	810	750	639	499	384	248	
	30	983	952	912	879	841	771	682	609	523	365
8¼%	10	860	601	271							
	15	927	791	617	476	308					
	20	957	878	777	695	597	418	188			
	25	974	925	863	813	753	643	502	387	251	
	30	983	953	914	882	844	774	685	613	527	368
8⅜%	10	861	603	272							
	15	927	793	620	478	310					
	20	958	880	780	697	600	420	189			
	25	974	927	865	815	756	646	505	390	253	
	30	984	954	915	884	847	778	689	616	530	372
8½%	10	861	604	273							
	15	928	794	622	480	312					
	20	958	881	782	700	603	423	191			
	25	975	928	867	818	759	649	508	392	255	
	30	984	955	917	886	849	781	693	620	534	375
8⅝%	10	862	606	274							
	15	929	796	624	482	314					
	20	959	883	784	703	606	426	192			
	25	975	929	869	820	762	653	512	395	257	
	30	985	956	919	888	852	784	696	624	538	378
8¾%	10	863	607	275							
	15	929	797	626	484	315					
	20	960	884	786	705	609	428	194			
	25	976	930	871	823	765	656	515	398	259	
	30	985	957	920	890	854	787	700	628	542	381
8⅞%	10	864	609	276							
	15	930	799	628	486	317					
	20	960	886	788	708	611	431	195			
	25	976	932	873	825	767	659	518	401	262	
	30	985	958	922	892	857	790	703	631	546	384
9 %	10	865	610	277							
	15	931	801	630	489	319					
	20	961	887	791	710	614	433	197			
	25	977	933	875	827	770	662	522	404	264	
	30	986	959	924	894	859	793	707	635	549	388
9⅛%	10	865	612	278							
	15	931	802	633	491	321					
	20	961	888	793	713	617	436	198			
	25	977	934	877	830	773	666	525	407	266	
	30	986	960	925	896	862	796	711	639	553	391
9¼%	10	866	613	280							
	15	932	804	635	493	322					
	20	962	890	795	715	620	439	200			
	25	978	935	879	832	776	669	528	410	268	
	30	986	961	927	898	864	799	714	643	557	394
9⅜%	10	867	615	281							
	15	933	805	637	495	324					
	20	962	891	797	718	622	441	201			
	25	978	936	881	834	778	672	531	413	271	
	30	987	962	928	900	866	802	717	646	560	397

Loan Progress Table

Showing the dollar balance remaining per $1,000 of loan

Interest Rate	Original Term	2	5	8	10	12	15	18	20	22	25
9½%	10	868	616	282							
	15	934	807	639	497	326					
	20	963	893	799	720	625	444	203			
	25	978	937	883	837	781	675	535	416	273	
	30	987	962	930	902	869	805	721	650	564	400
9⅝%	10	869	618	283							
	15	934	809	641	499	328					
	20	964	894	801	723	628	446	205			
	25	979	938	885	839	784	678	538	419	275	
	30	987	963	931	904	871	808	724	653	568	404
9¾%	10	869	619	284							
	15	935	810	643	501	330					
	20	964	895	803	725	631	449	206			
	25	979	940	886	841	786	681	541	422	277	
	30	988	964	933	906	873	811	728	657	571	407
9⅞%	10	870	621	285							
	15	936	812	645	504	331					
	20	965	897	805	728	633	452	208			
	25	980	941	888	843	789	685	544	425	279	
	30	988	965	934	908	876	814	731	661	575	410
10 %	10	871	622	286							
	15	936	813	647	506	333					
	20	965	898	807	730	636	454	209			
	25	980	942	890	846	792	688	547	428	282	
	30	988	966	935	909	878	817	734	664	578	413
10⅛%	10	872	623	288							
	15	937	815	649	508	335					
	20	966	899	810	733	639	457	211			
	25	980	943	892	848	794	691	551	431	284	
	30	989	967	937	911	880	819	738	668	582	416
10¼%	10	872	625	289							
	15	937	816	651	510	337					
	20	966	901	812	735	641	459	212			
	25	981	944	893	850	797	694	554	433	286	
	30	989	967	938	913	882	822	741	671	585	419
10⅜%	10	873	626	290							
	15	938	818	654	512	338					
	20	967	902	814	738	644	462	214			
	25	981	945	895	852	799	697	557	436	288	
	30	989	968	939	915	884	825	744	674	589	422
10½%	10	874	628	291							
	15	939	819	656	514	340					
	20	967	903	816	740	647	464	215			
	25	982	946	897	854	802	700	560	439	290	
	30	989	969	941	916	886	828	747	678	592	426
10⅝%	10	875	629	292							
	15	939	821	658	516	342					
	20	968	904	818	742	649	467	217			
	25	982	947	898	856	804	703	563	442	293	
	30	990	970	942	918	888	830	750	681	596	429
10¾%	10	875	631	293							
	15	940	822	660	519	344					
	20	968	906	820	745	652	470	218			
	25	982	948	900	858	807	706	566	445	295	
	30	990	970	943	919	890	833	754	685	599	432

Loan Amortization And Loan Progress Tables

Loan Progress Table

Showing the dollar balance remaining per $1,000 of loan

Interest Rate	Original Term	2	5	8	10	12	15	18	20	22	25
10⅞%	10	876	632	294							
	15	941	824	662	521	345					
	20	969	907	821	747	654	472	220			
	25	983	949	901	860	809	709	569	448	297	
	30	990	971	944	921	892	835	757	688	603	435
11 %	10	877	634	296							
	15	941	825	664	523	347					
	20	969	908	823	749	657	475	221			
	25	983	950	903	862	812	712	572	451	299	
	30	990	972	945	923	894	838	760	691	606	438
11⅛%	10	878	635	297							
	15	942	827	666	525	349					
	20	970	909	825	752	660	477	223			
	25	983	950	905	864	814	714	575	454	302	
	30	991	972	947	924	896	840	763	695	610	441
11¼%	10	878	636	298							
	15	942	828	668	527	351					
	20	970	911	827	754	662	480	225			
	25	984	951	906	866	816	717	579	456	304	
	30	991	973	948	926	898	843	766	698	613	444
11⅜%	10	879	638	299							
	15	943	829	670	529	352					
	20	971	912	829	756	665	482	226			
	25	984	952	908	868	819	720	582	459	306	
	30	991	974	949	927	900	845	769	701	616	447
11½%	10	880	639	300							
	15	944	831	672	531	354					
	20	971	913	831	759	667	485	228			
	25	984	953	909	870	821	723	585	462	308	
	30	991	974	950	929	902	848	772	704	620	450
11⅝%	10	881	641	301							
	15	944	832	674	533	356					
	20	971	914	833	761	670	487	229			
	25	985	954	911	872	823	726	588	465	310	
	30	992	975	951	930	903	850	775	708	623	453
11¾%	10	881	642	302							
	15	945	834	676	535	358					
	20	972	915	835	763	672	490	231			
	25	985	955	912	874	826	729	591	468	313	
	30	992	975	952	931	905	852	777	711	626	456
11⅞%	10	882	644	304							
	15	945	835	678	537	360					
	20	972	916	837	765	675	492	232			
	25	985	956	913	876	828	731	594	471	315	
	30	992	976	953	933	907	855	780	714	630	459
12 %	10	883	645	305							
	15	946	837	680	540	361					
	20	973	917	838	767	677	495	234			
	25	986	957	915	878	830	734	597	473	317	
	30	992	977	954	934	909	857	783	717	633	462
12⅛%	10	884	648	307							
	15	947	839	684	544	365					
	20	974	920	842	772	682	500	237			
	25	986	958	918	881	835	740	603	479	322	
	30	993	978	956	937	912	862	789	723	639	468

Loan Progress Table

Showing the dollar balance remaining per $1,000 of loan

Interest Rate	Original Term	2	5	8	10	12	15	18	20	22	25
12½%	10	886	651	309							
	15	948	842	688	548	368					
	20	974	922	845	776	687	505	240			
	25	987	960	920	885	839	745	608	485	326	
	30	993	979	958	939	915	866	794	729	646	474
12¾%	10	887	653	312							
	15	949	845	692	552	372					
	20	975	924	849	780	692	510	243			
	25	987	961	923	888	843	750	614	490	330	
	30	993	980	960	942	918	870	800	735	652	480
13 %	10	888	656	314							
	15	950	847	695	556	376					
	20	976	926	852	785	697	515	246			
	25	988	963	926	891	847	755	620	496	335	
	30	994	981	962	944	922	874	805	741	658	486
13¼%	10	890	659	316							
	15	952	850	699	560	379					
	20	977	928	856	789	702	520	250			
	25	988	964	928	895	851	760	626	501	339	
	30	994	982	963	946	924	878	810	747	664	492
13½%	10	891	662	319							
	15	953	853	703	564	383					
	20	977	930	859	793	707	525	253			
	25	989	965	930	898	855	765	631	507	343	
	30	994	983	965	949	927	882	815	752	670	498
13¾%	10	892	665	321							
	15	954	855	707	568	386					
	20	978	932	862	797	711	530	256			
	25	989	967	933	901	859	770	637	512	348	
	30	995	983	967	951	930	886	820	758	676	504
14 %	10	894	667	323							
	15	955	858	711	572	390					
	20	979	934	865	801	716	534	259			
	25	990	968	935	904	863	775	642	517	352	
	30	995	984	968	953	933	890	824	763	682	509
14¼%	10	895	670	326							
	15	956	860	714	576	393					
	20	980	936	868	805	720	539	262			
	25	990	969	937	907	867	780	648	523	357	
	30	995	985	970	955	935	893	829	768	688	515
14½%	10	896	673	328							
	15	957	863	718	580	397					
	20	980	937	871	809	725	544	265			
	25	991	970	939	910	870	785	653	528	361	
	30	996	986	971	957	938	897	834	774	694	520
14¾%	10	898	675	330							
	15	957	865	722	584	400					
	20	981	939	874	812	729	549	268			
	25	991	972	941	912	874	789	658	533	365	
	30	996	987	972	959	940	900	838	779	699	526
15 %	10	899	678	333							
	15	958	868	725	588	404					
	20	981	941	877	816	734	554	272			
	25	991	973	943	915	877	794	664	538	369	
	30	996	987	973	960	942	903	842	784	705	532

ABOUT THE AUTHORS

Don DeBat, award-winning assistant managing editor of real estate for the *Chicago Sun-Times,* has covered the mortgage, finance, and housing markets for nearly two decades. He is widely known for his consumer-oriented newspaper columns.

In 1987 DeBat's story "Banking on Home Equity" was cited for excellence in a national contest sponsored by the National Association Of Real Estate Editors. The article, which explained the consumer pitfalls of home-equity loans, also won first place for financial feature writing in a contest sponsored by the Financial Institutions Marketing Association.

In 1983 DeBat's story "The Mortgage Race" won first place in the consumer category of the National Association of Real Estate Editors writing contest. The article outlined 12 ways to finance the purchase of a home.

In 1982 "The ARMs Race" pointed out the drawbacks of financing a home with an adjustable-rate mortgage, and "The Perils of Creative Finance" delved into the pitfalls of buying a home on contract with short-term balloon financing. The articles won national citations from the Real Estate Educators Association and the National Association of Real Estate Editors.

A real estate investor, DeBat has renovated and restored two vintage homes in Chicago, and he once headed a community group that won historic landmark district status for a city neighborhood. DeBat received his master's degree in 1968 and a bachelor's degree in 1966 from the University of Missouri School of Journalism in Columbia.

Thomas A. Kelly holds a master of management degree from Northwestern University's Kellogg Graduate School of Management with concentrations in finance and marketing.

His financial expertise contributed to a *Chicago Sun-Times* series inspecting private mortgage insurance. The series was first runner-up in the 1985 National Association of Real Estate Editors contest and won the 1986 feature reporting award from the Financial Institutions Marketing Association.

Kelly, who also holds a bachelor of science degree from Northwestern's Medill School of Journalism, is the real estate editor of the *Chicago Sun-Times*.

INDEX

Acceleration clause, 61–62
Adjustable rate mortgages (ARMs), 5–6, 17, 102–3
   advantages of, 103
   assumability of, 102
   bad reputation of, 104–5
   comparison of fixed-rate loan with, 155–56
   conversion of, 110–11
   disadvantages of, 103
   fluctuating market of, 105–6
   functioning of, 104
   interest rate in, 102
   one-year ARM, 108–9
   payment changes in, 102
   popularity of, 18
   rate adjustments in, 102
   recommended for, 102
   at savings and loans, 9
   standardized requirements, 106–7
   term of loan in, 102
   three-year and five-year ARMs, 109–10
   variances of, 107–8
AFL-CIO union pension fund, 12
Allen, Michael L., 65, 110
Amortization, negative, 107, 113–14
Annual percentage rate (APR), 25, 63–64
   computing, 65
Application fee, 154

Appraisal, 25
Appraisal fee, 154
APR. *See* Annual percentage rate (APR)
ARMs. *See* Adjustable rate mortgages (ARMs)

Balloon loans, 6, 15–16, 130, 131–32, 133
Bell Federal Savings, 82, 142
Biweekly mortgage, 5, 79–80
   advantages of, 80
   assumability of, 79
   challenges and opportunities with, 82–83
   disadvantages of, 80, 83
   as imported from Canada, 81–82
   interest rate in, 79
   maximum loan amount for, 79
   payment changes in, 79
   payoff of, 81
   rate adjustments in, 79
   recommended for, 79
   term of loan in, 79
Brunner, Bob, 82, 141
Building maintenance, 60
Bush, George, 18
Butler, Merrill, 17
Buydowns, 136, 143–44

Canada, origination of biweekly loan in, 81–82

172 THE MORTGAGE MANUAL

Century 21, 151
Child/investor, negative cash flow for, in Grannie Maes, 123-24
Citicorp Loan Corporation, 151
Closing, time for, 159
Closing costs
  deed recording, 27
  document preparation, 27
  on FHA loan, 88-89
  initial mortgage payment, 26
  lawyer fees, 27
  loan application fee, 25, 26
  points, 25
  prepaid homeowner's insurance, 27
  private mortgage insurance, 26
  property survey, 26
  prorated property taxes, 27
  recording taxes, 27
  summary of, 27-28
  title search and insurance, 26
Coldwell Banker Real Estate, 151
Commercial banks, as source of mortgage money, 9-10
Computerized mortgage hunting, 149-51
Contract sales, 6, 130, 134-35, 161
Cost-of-funds index, 104, 109
Creative financing, 130
  balloon loans, 6, 15-16, 130, 131-32, 133
  buydowns, 136, 143-44
  contract sales, 6, 130, 134-35, 161
  mortgage assumption, 132-33
  prepaying mortgage, 68, 83, 137-38
  purchase-money mortgages, 135
  second mortgages, 130
  seller-held second mortgages, 135-36

  zero percent financing, 138-39
Credit report, 25, 54, 154
  time required for, 47
Credit requirements, tightening of, 56
Credit unions, as source for mortgage money, 11-12
Culver, Curt, 24

Deed recording, 27
Deed restrictions, 60
Deregulation, impact of, on fixed-rate mortgages, 17
Direct endorsement, 85
Disclosure rules, 64-66
Discount points, 88-89
Document preparation, 27
Down payment
  for conventional loan, 22
  effect of size of, 157-58
  for FHA loan, 22, 71, 87
  help from parents with, 141-43
  on jumbo conventional loan, 72
  for loan at savings and loan, 8
  for mortgage loan at commercial bank, 10
  sources for, 22-23
  on VA loan, 71, 94, 95
Due-on-sale clauses, 62-63, 133
Dwars, Peter, 99

Elderly, loans for. See Grannie Maes; Reverse equity loans
Employment verification, 55
Equity sharing, 146-47
ERA, 151
Evidence of good title, 60

Family Backed Mortgage Association, 124
Fannie Mae. See Federal National Mortgage Association (FNMA)

Index 173

Federal Home Loan Bank Board (FHLBB), 126
Federal Home Loan Mortgage Corporation (FHLMC), 9, 13–14, 52
Federal Housing Administration (FHA), 16. *See also* FHA loans
   pilot program for reverse equity loans, 126–28
Federal National Mortgage Association (FNMA), 13, 52, 107
Federal Reserve Board, 20
FHA loans, 5, 10, 16, 50, 84–85, 113, 160
   advantages of, 85
   closing fees, 88–89
   disadvantages of, 85–86
   discount points on, 88–89
   down payment for, 22, 71, 87
   government insurance of, 86–87
   interest rate in, 84
   loan origination fee, 88
   maximum loan amount for, 84
   payment changes in, 84
   rate adjustments in, 84
   recommended for, 84
   setting standards for, 89–90
   as source of mortgage money, 84
   term of loan in, 84
15-year, fixed-rate loans, 33, 73–74
   advantages of, 74
   assumability of, 73
   comparison of, with 30-year fixed-rate loan, 49–50, 156–57
   comparison of payments, 77
   disadvantages of, 74
   drawbacks of, 78
   equity growth, 75
   growth in popularity of, 20
   interest rate in, 73
   interest saved in, 76–77
   maximum loan amount for, 73
   payment changes in, 73
   popularity of, 75
   principal payoff in, 74–75
   rate adjustments in, 73
   recommended for, 73
   term of loan in, 73
Fixed-rate mortgage loan, 4–5. *See also* 15-year, fixed-rate loans; 30-year, fixed-rate loans
   comparison of, with adjustable-rate mortgage, 155–56
   conversion of ARMs to, 110–11
   decline in, 16–17
   history of, 18–20
Freddie Mac. *See* Federal Home Loan Mortgage Corporation (FHLMC)

Ginnie Mae. *See* Government National Mortgage Association (GNMA)
Government National Mortgage Association (GNMA), 13
Graduated-payment loans, 87, 112–14
   assumability of, 112
   interest rate in, 112
   payment changes in, 112
   rate adjustments in, 112
   recommended for, 112, 113
   term of loan in, 112
Graduated-payment mortgages (GPMs), 6, 157
Gramm-Rudman Act, 20
Grannie Maes, 120–21, 160
   advantages of, 121

annuity payments in, 122
disadvantages of, 121
drawbacks in, 123
  costly fees, 124-25
  negative cash flow for child/investor, 123-24
  parental allowance, 124
  sibling partnerships, 124
  tax liability, 124
  solving cash flow problem, 121-25
Growing equity mortgage, 6, 114-15
  advantages of, 115
  assumability of, 115
  disadvantages of, 115-16
  interest rate in, 115
  need for rising income in, 116-17
  payment changes in, 115
  rate adjustments in, 115
  recommended for, 115
  term of loan in, 115

Home budget worksheet, 39-40
Home inspector, 23, 159
Home ownership, decline in, 3
Home ownership costs
  income tax savings, 41-44
  monthly payments, 35-38
Home-owning majority, 4
Housing costs, monthly, 35-38

Income, proof of, 55
Income tax savings, computing, 40-44
Initial mortgage payment, 26
Interest rate
  affordability of, 1
  locking in, 26, 155
  volatility of, 15-20

Jumbo conventional loan, 71-72
  down payment on, 72

Lawyer. *See* Real estate attorney
Loan amortization tables, 162-63
  15-year, fixed-rate loan, 163-64
  30-year, fixed-rate loan, 163
Loan application fee, 25, 159
Loan commitments, 11
  expiration of, 11, 47
Loan origination fee, 26, 154
Loan progress tables, 164-68
Low-documentation mortgages, 48

Marder, Thomas O., 75
May, Judith V., 126
Meyers, Gary S., 54, 64-65
Moltz, Marshall J., 45, 46, 58, 61, 131, 132, 135, 136
Monthly mortgage payment, calculation of, 29-32
Mortgage
  average amount spent for, 1-3
  calculating monthly payment for, 29-32
  computing affordability of, 152
  costs of, 154
  looking for, 153
  qualifying for, 28-29
  shopping for, 45-53, 153-54
  sources of money for, 7-14
Mortgage application process
  bank accounts, 55
  checkbook in, 54
  copies of all documents, 56
  credit cards, 55
  credit report, 54
  employment verification, 55
  outstanding loans, 55
  previous loans, 56
  proof of income, 55
  questionable debts, 56
Mortgage approval, speeding up of, 54-56, 159
Mortgage assumption, 130, 132-33

Mortgage bankers and brokers
  criticisms of, 11
  as source of mortgage money,
    10–11
Mortgage bond financing, 97–98
  advantages of, 98
  assumability of, 97
  disadvantages of, 98
  example of, 98–99
  interest rate in, 97
  mortgage amount, 97
  payment changes in, 97
  rate adjustments in, 97
  reason for low rates in, 99–100
  recommended for, 97
  term of loan in, 97
  U.S. Treasury opposition to,
    100–1
Mortgage contingency provisions
  59–60
Mortgage fees. *See* Closing costs
Mortgage Guaranty Insurance
  Corporation (MGIC), 24, 65
Mortgage Power, 151

National Credit Union
  Administration, 12
National Housing Act (1974), 113
Negative amortization, 107,
  113–14

Oil prices, effect of, on interest
  rates, 20
$100,000 home, mortgage
  payments and income needed
  to buy, 2

Parental aid, 140–41
  co-signing loan, 144–45
  with down payment, 141–43
  emotional considerations,
    147–48
  equity sharing, 146–47
  holding mortgage, 145–46
  points at closing, 144
  rate buydown, 143–44
Payment cap, 109
Payment shock, 69
Pension funds, as source for
  mortgage money, 12
Pincich, Sam, 141, 142, 143
Plat of survey, 60
Podbelski, David, 89
Points, 25, 154, 158
Prepaid homeowner's insurance,
  27
Prepayments, of mortgage, 8, 68,
  83, 137–38
Principal, interest, taxes, and
  insurance (PITI), 2, 29
Principal and interest (PI)
  on 15-year mortgage, 33
  on 30-year mortgage, 34
Private Mortgage Insurance
  (PMI), 23–25, 26, 154, 157–58
Property survey, 26
  plat of, 60
Property taxes, 154
  prorated, 27
Prudential, 151
Prudential-Bache Securities,
  reverse mortgage
  development by, 128–29
Puntillo, Richard, 125
Purchase-money mortgages, 135

Real estate attorney, 154
  fees for, 27
  need for, 58–61, 159
Recording taxes, 27, 154
Regulation Z, 64
Reinlein, Karl, 75, 78
Restrictions of record, 60
Reverse-equity mortgages, 6,
  125–26
  assumability of, 125
  FHA pilot program, 126–28

line-of-credit option, 127
tenure option, 127
term option, 127
interest rate in, 125
payment changes in, 125
private programs for, 128–29
rate adjustments in, 125
recommended for, 125
term of loan in, 125
Rider. *See also* Sales contract clauses
for home inspection, 23
Right to inspect, 60
Rosen, Kenneth, 124
Rowan, Robert G., 142

Sales contract clauses, 57–58. *See also* Rider
acceleration clause, 61–62
building maintenance, 60
due-on-sale clauses, 62–63
evidence of good title, 60
mortgage contingency provisions, 59–60
plat of survey, 60
restrictions of record, 60
right to inspect, 60
subject to attorney approval, 58–59
tax proration, 58, 59
warranty against defects, 61
SAM. *See* Shared-appreciation mortgage (SAM)
Sanderman, Maurice, 139
Savings and loan associations, as source of mortgage money, 7, 8–9, 153
Secondary market
Federal Home Loan Mortgage Corporation, 9, 13–14, 24, 52
Federal National Mortgage Association, 13, 52
Government National Mortgage Association, 13
as source of mortgage money, 12–14
Second mortgages, 130
seller-held, 135–36
Seller-held balloon loans, 130
Seller-held second mortgages, 135–36
Shanahan, Edmond, 82
Shared-appreciation mortgage (SAM), 117–19
assumability of, 118
interest rate in, 118
payment changes in, 118
rate adjustments in, 118
recommended for, 118
term of loan in, 118
Shared-housing situations, 52
Sonneck, Robert, 101
Sundance Homes, 138–39
Survey, 26
plat of, 60

Tahnan Home Mortgage Corp., 81–82, 141, 142–43
Taxes and homeowners' insurance payments (T&I), 2
Tax-exempt bond financing, 99
Tax prorations, 58, 59
T-bill index, 104
30-year, fixed-rate mortgage loan, 67–68
advantages of, 68
assumability of, 67
comparison of, with 15-year loan, 49–50, 156–57
comparison of payments, 77
disadvantages of, 68
interest rate in, 67
loan maximums in, 71–72
maximum loan amount for, 67

payment changes in, 67
payments for principal and interest on, 34
rate adjustments in, 67
recommended for, 67, 70–71
stable monthly payments in, 68–70
term of loan in, 67
Title commitment policy, 60
Title insurance, 26, 154
Title insurance company, 26
Title insurance policy, 60
Title search, 26, 154
Truth-in-Lending Act, 63, 64, 65

United Air Lines Employees' Credit Union, 12
U.S. Treasury, opposition of, to mortgage bond financing, 100–1

VA loan, 5, 10, 91–92, 160–61
advantages of, 92
assumability of, 91
disadvantages of, 92–93
down payment on, 71, 94, 95
eligibility for, 93–94
fees for, 95–96
interest rate in, 91
maximum loan guarantee, 91
payment changes in, 91
rate adjustments in, 91
recommended for, 91
term of loan in, 91, 94–95
Veterans' Home Loan Indemnity Act, 95

Warranty against defects, 61

Yuppie mortgage, 79. *See also* Biweekly mortgage

Zellars, John B., 105
Zero percent financing, 138–39

These other Contemporary real estate classics are available in your local bookstore or by mail. To order directly, return the coupon below with a check, money order, or credit card payment to: Contemporary Books, Department BSD, 180 North Michigan Avenue, Chicago, Illinois 60601. Or call (312) 782-9181 for quantity discount information.

....

Title/Author	SBN	Price	Quantity
House Inspection: A Buyer's Guide by Dale Chaney and Jeff Miller	4838-7	$8.95	_____
How to Buy a House When You're Cash Poor by Vanessa A. Bush	4834-4	$5.95	_____
Selling Your House Without a Broker by Dale Chaney and Mary Beth Libbey	4833-6	$5.95	_____
Twenty Proven Ways to Profit from Real Estate by R. J. Turner	4256-7	$8.95	_____
		Subtotal	_____

Please add $1.00 postage for the first book
and $.50 postage for each additional book.   _____

Illinois residents add 7% sales tax; California
residents add 6%.   _____

Total Price   _____

_____ Enclosed is my check/money order payable to Contemporary Books.
_____ Bill my ☐ VISA ☐ MasterCard Number_____

Expiration Date_____Signature_____

Please allow four to six weeks for delivery.

MM1089